Cozy Coastal Knits

Rosann Fleischauer

STACKPOLE BOOKS

Essex, Connecticut
Blue Ridge Summit, Pennsylvania

STACKPOLE BOOKS

An imprint of Globe Pequot, the trade division of The Rowman & Littlefield Publishing Group, Inc.
4501 Forbes Blvd., Ste. 200
Lanham, MD 20706
www.rowman.com

Distributed by NATIONAL BOOK NETWORK
800-462-6420

British Library Cataloguing in Publication Information available

Library of Congress Cataloging-in-Publication Data available

Names: Fleischauer, Rosann, 1969- author.
Title: Cozy coastal knits / Rosann Fleischauer.
Description: First edition. | Essex, Connecticut : Stackpole Books, [2023]
Identifiers: LCCN 2023001782 (print) | LCCN 2023001783 (ebook) | ISBN 9780811772167 (paperback) | ISBN 9780811772174 (epub)
Subjects: LCSH: Knitting--Patterns. | Knitwear.
Classification: LCC TT825 .F558 2023 (print) | LCC TT825 (ebook) | DDC 746.43/2041--dc23/eng/20230223
LC record available at https://lccn.loc.gov/2023001782
LC ebook record available at https://lccn.loc.gov/2023001783

♾™ The paper used in this publication meets the minimum requirements of American National Standard for Information Sciences—Permanence of Paper for Printed Library Materials, ANSI/NISO Z39.48-1992.

First Edition

To my mom, Barbara Palermo, who instilled in me a love of the coast and just might be the only person who keeps a kite in the Jeep for last-minute beach excursions, "because you never know when you just need to go fly a kite."

And

To my husband, Erik. Had you not bought a boat, I might never have picked up a pair of knitting needles.

All my love,
Rosann

Contents

Patterns

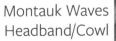

Introduction

As the waves began to settle down before the sunset over the Gulf in Key West, it occurred to me: this was the perfect spot to knit. Yes, right there, gently swaying back and forth in a hammock held aloft by two palm trees—that's where I was when I pulled out a scarf from my tote bag and decided to knit through my jet lag. After a few rounds of mojitos and knitting the most delicious hand-dyed green cashmere Cape Cod had to offer the last time we were in port, my mind began to wander and capture the serenity of the moment. The result: every time I put on the scarf to fend off the bitter damp days of a New England winter, I think of that relaxing vacation and the way the breeze gently rocked the hammock, stitch after enjoyable stitch.

In an effort to expand the joyful memories that scarf created, I became more diligent about bringing a project along on all our trips. I knit a hat round after round as we cycled from Key Largo to Marathon, using yarn I found in La Jolla, California; and knit a sweater while exploring the Eastern Shore of Maryland, for which I used a wonderful alpaca I found in Manhattan.

My closet became a cozy knit scrapbook of my coastal travels. As my collection grew, I began thinking of ways to help others build their own collections of useful, timeless, fashionable mementos that will never go out of style. The result is this book: a compilation of projects with classic lines using simple techniques so you, too, can create a living collection of memories. No immediate travel plans? Let your imagination take you on a journey; pick out yarns that evoke happiness as you create your own collection of useful fiber art.

I designed the patterns in this book to be easy to follow and help you build a sophisticated wardrobe as your time permits. As with sailing, knitting is not about the ending—it is about the journey. Join me as we knit from coast to coast creating flattering, suitable, timeless, and memorable pieces.

My goal is to inspire you to create something beautiful and meaningful that you can enjoy for years to come, whether wearing it yourself or enjoying the company of people in your life lucky to own something you knit for them.

I hope you enjoy this book and use it as a guide to create a cozy knit selection of mementos. Make notes in the margins, use a postcard as a bookmark, enjoy the journey. Write down what you loved about each skein, stitch, and finished object to weave together your own book of memories.

Tools to Make Your Knitting Life a Little Easier

$\mathcal{T}$he best tools are those you find useful to make your precious creative time more enjoyable. Here are some basics to get you started on your fiber journey.

NEEDLES

Needles are the most basic knitting tool. You will want to find pairs that suit your lifestyle and the projects on which you are embarking. In general I suggest circular needles because they can be used to work wider pieces of knitted fabric than straight needles, and are less prone to breakage than straight needles.

The basics to consider when selecting needles are as follows.

Tips

The tip of a knitting needle is where most of your work will take place. A smooth blunt tip may suit one yarn or stitch more comfortably than a pointy stiletto tip. When swatching for a project you may even find that the tip impacts the experience of working with a given yarn and the gauge of your work.

Tips of six different US size 6/4 mm needles. Notice the shape of each is slightly different. Some are more pointy, others have a blunt edge, and even the length of the tapered section varies on each. The geometry of the tip combined with the material(s) from which the needle is made will impact your gauge.

Material—wood, plastic, or metal

Depending on the texture of a given yarn, you may find needles made from one material to be easier to use than another. Wooden needles tend to provide a bit more grip to hold the yarn as you work and warm to the touch. The wood and its finish will affect the amount of friction of a given needle and will impact your work. Most needles tend to be made of bamboo or maple. For a luxurious straight wooden option, Brittany needles are available in walnut. Metal needles tend to be more slick than their wooden counterparts and grip the yarn less as they are used to work the yarn. Plastic needles tend to perform more similarly to wooden needles than to metal needles.

Pro Tip: If your gauge is a little off, sometimes changing from one needle material to another in the same size needle will yield the result you desire for a given yarn.

Needle shape—square or round shaft

The shape of the needle will influence how you hold it. While round shaft needles are more common, square shafts are also available in both straight and circular configurations.

Pro Tip: If you have a lot of knitting time, you may find it helpful to have multiple projects in process simultaneously, each with a different size and type of needle. Working with different-sized needles will require a slightly different grip for each and will reduce hand strain.

Addi sells an interesting hybrid metal needle, the Rocket 2 Squared, which features gently chamfered corners that make them easier to work with for those of us who may spend a few extra hours a day with needles in hand or those who are looking for an alternative shape for more comfortable knitting. If you look at the Rocket 2 Squared, how you would possibly get consistent gauge might not make sense until you try it. Remember, most of your gauge is worked out at the tips of the needles (not along the shaft), so as long as the stitches comfortably sit on the needle, it's really all about the top inch of the needles themselves.

Weight

Some needles are heavier than others and, depending on your knitting style, you may find it's easier to use a type that is heavier than another. The weight of a set of needles will influence how you grip them, so over time your preference may change.

Length

Straight and circular needles are available in different lengths. Straight needles are typically available in lengths of 6 to 12 inches; occasionally I have found 14-inch sets. I prefer straight needles when I am working on a sweater in the comfort of my own studio, so I do buy the longer ones when I find them.

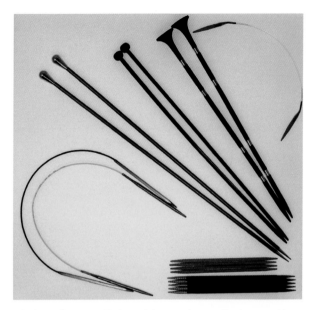

Clockwise from top: Furls straight wooden needles in a combination of wood and metal, Clover 9-inch circular bamboo needle, Knitters' Pride Carbonz double-pointed needles, Brittany maple double-pointed needles, Addi Turbo nickel-plated circular needle, Kollage Square circular metal needle, Signature Needle Arts 14-inch straight metal needles, and vintage walnut needles with a square shaft. Each provides a slightly different knitting experience.

Double-pointed straight needles (abbreviated "DPNs") are typically sold in sets of four or five. They are traditionally used for knitting in the round. Double-pointed needles provide the opportunity to work comfortably in the round when working a tight number of stitches, such as for the crown of a hat or cuff of a sleeve.

Pro Tip: When working on a cable, a single double-pointed needle may be used in lieu of a cable needle.

Circular needle lengths are typically measured by the overall length from tip to tip. However, there are very few agreed-upon standards in the knitting industry. The length of the needle shaft will impact the comfort of holding a circular needle in your hands and the types of things you can easily knit with the circular needle. When looking at circular needles it is important to consider the material, length, and the way in which the cable is joined to the needle. The needle and cable are typically not the same material and, as a result, at the point where they meet there is a junction that may or may not be well engineered.

Interchangeable needle sets are available, which allow you to adjust the length of the circular needle by using different cables or attaching them to each other for even greater variety.

If it were not confusing enough, one final consideration when choosing circular needles is the cable itself. Each manufacturer has a slightly different approach to cable construction; some types are more flexible and easy to work with than others. In the photo of needle types, notice that the Clover needle has a plastic cable, the Kollage has a composite cable, and the Addi has a plastic-coated cable.

Interchangeable needle sets can be misleading. They are not a "one-size-fits-all" solution. For example, attaching a pair of 5-inch needles to an 8-inch cord will yield an 18-inch circular needle; however, it will not work well because the length of the needles versus the cord is too close to allow you to use the circular needle comfortably. A pair of 3.5-inch needles on the same 8-inch cord will be usable; thus the reason for the availability of interchangeable sets with different-length needles, like those from Lykke and Addi.

To further complicate the decision-making process when choosing a set of interchangeable needles or a fixed-length circular needle, there is the consideration of twist. Some cables spin freely where they meet the needle, others do not. Depending upon your personal style of knitting, it may be easier to use one type than another, so consider swivel-ability too when looking at circular needles.

Pro Tips:

o   When choosing interchangeable needle sets, consider the style of construction where the cable meets the needle. The smoother the point at which they meet, the easier it will be slide your work over it. Each manufacturer has its own way of joining the cables to the needles. Some fit together better than others, and some require a specific tool to join them.

o   Ask people what they like, borrow needles from others to try them out, and ask at your local yarn stores, where you might be able to "test drive" a few different versions before making a purchase.

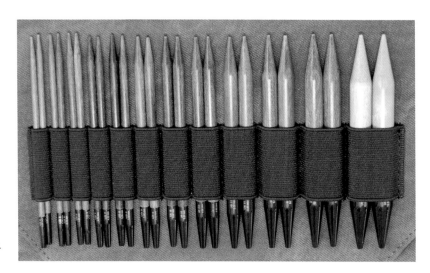

It can be convenient to have a set of circular needles with interchangeable cords of variable length, such as these Lykke needles.

GAUGE MEASUREMENT DEVICES

Gauge determines how large your finished object will be over a specified number of stitches. Measuring your gauge is critical for fitted garments, so it pays to have an accurate tool available. Gauge measuring tools are available at a range of price points and in various styles. Personally, I like to smile every time I reach for a tool, so I have three on my desk: a classic metal one from Susan Bates, and two beautiful wooden ones from Katrinkles. The smaller one is useful for preliminary gauge studies. The larger one provides a more complete picture of final gauge as I near the end of a swatching exercise.

Pro Tip: The larger the swatch, the more accurate your gauge measurement.

NEEDLE GAUGE

As a beginner, I did not think I needed a needle gauge. My rationale was pretty simple: the little bags in which the needles are sold have a number on them, and so do the needles themselves. Over time I realized that the little plastic bags fell apart, and the numbers became more difficult to read. After several failed attempts to get gauge on what I thought were three different-sized needles, I got a needle gauge and discovered in fact the three were precisely the same diameter shaft, which is why I got the exact same gauge on all three needles. So long story short, keep a needle gauge in your bag. It will come in handy someday. It's really difficult to see the difference in the circumference of two needles that may differ by only .5 mm.

A gauge swatch ruler makes quick work of measuring your swatch. When swatching my final one or two yarns, I prefer to make a 6- to 8-inch/15- to 20-centimeter swatch rather than the standard 4 inches/10 centimeters, so the larger gauge measuring tool comes in quite handy.

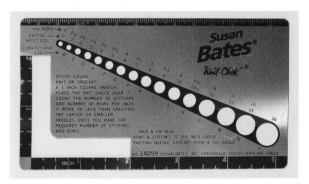

This classic tool from Susan Bates for measuring gauge and needle sizes is a budget-friendly tool available at most big-box craft stores.

Over time, unless the label on a needle is laser etched, it will become difficult to read. A needle gauge takes the mystery out of which needle is which.

For a nautical twist, Katrinkles has the Whale Knitting Needle Gauge. For dog lovers, there is a Dachshund option.

ROW COUNTER

Most patterns are written in rows or rounds. To keep track of the row or round count, add a row counter to your project bag. Finish a row, advance the counter—easy. The two I use most often are a simple one that sits on my needles when knitting away from home, and an adorable one that sits on the table next to my favorite chair in my studio because it's too darn cute to put in a bag and stow next to the chair.

POM-POM MAKER

Granted, none of the projects in this book have pom-poms; however, as any knitter knows, it is rare that a project is completed with absolutely no left-overs so there are likely some random bits of yarn rolling around your den or project bag that could be reimagined as the finishing touch on another project. One way to keep leftovers at bay is to repurpose leftover yarn. Pom-poms and tassels are two ways I repurpose yarn. They are useful to top off projects, in lieu of a bow on a wrapped gift, for an impromptu "snowball" fight, to make small toys, and to decorate a wreath form. Keep a pom-pom maker in your bag to occupy non-knitters on long car trips, or tucked into a leftovers basket at home so they are paired and at the ready.

CHEAT SHEETS FOR KNITTERS

No pattern is perfectly suited to every situation. A modification here or there will always arise. To keep track of changes on paper patterns, I keep a couple pencils in my project bag so one is always close at hand for jotting down what I had to change for a particular project. These notes are critical if making two of the same thing that need to match each other, like sleeves or socks.

Pro Tip: After making notes on a pattern, scan them or take a picture of the notes so they are available at a future date.

For working on the road, the row counter on the left is perfectly serviceable and available at most big-box arts and crafts stores. On the right, the adorable row-counting little sheep from Katrinkles is my favorite. Every time I use it, I cannot help but smile as I pick it up and advance a row. Try it, you'll see!

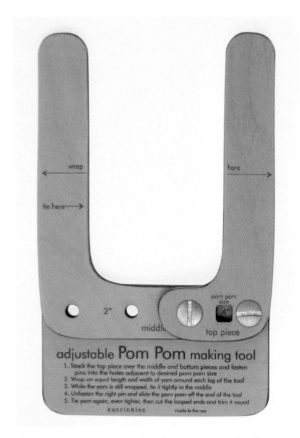

The engineer in me marveled at this pom-pom maker from Katrinkles, so simple and easy to use. Even the directions are close at hand for your pom-pom-making assistant to follow without having to interrupt you while you knit.

To take your notes up a notch while preserving the paper pattern itself, use a trick I learned in architecture school. Rather than mark up the paper pattern, place it into a plastic sleeve and make your notes directly on the sleeve using a permanent marker or dry-erase marker, depending on whether you think you'll want the notes in the future. I tend toward the permanent option as I typically make several items from the same pattern, and having the notes close at hand is exceptionally helpful.

When working with an electronic pattern, use an online editing tool. For most pattern formats, there is an editing or commenting capability built into the display tool. Use your favorite internet search engine to find out how to pair your electronic pattern format with a tool through which you can record comments. On my iPad I use iBooks, wherein I can add comments by selecting text in a pdf and choosing the highlight function from the pop-up menu to literally highlight the selected text or add a comment, not unlike a little electronic Post-it® note.

For a pattern that repeats itself over a few rows, add a short note directly onto the RS and WS of the piece to help you keep track of your progress. This can be a simple set of markers labeled "RS" and "WS," or a short set of instructions to yourself like "RS—Sl1, k1" attached to a stitch marker. I find this method particularly useful if I have a few different works in progress on the needles.

For tricky stitch patterns like the Kitchener stitch, I am building a small arsenal of tools to combat my inability to remember them. My favorites are the sturdy little wooden laser-etched squares from our fellow knitters at Katrinkles. I pick them up whenever I find them at a local yarn store or festival. They are handy little helpers, lightweight and easily attached to the handle of a knitting bag to keep my work on track when I simply cannot remember something as routine as a wrap-and-turn or complicated like the Kitchener stitch.

For those steps that are not quite laser etched in my brain, these laser-engraved instructional tip cards available from Katrinkles make a big difference.

Pro Tip: Small notions like the laser-etched tools discussed here make excellent gifts. They are easy to transport, easy to mail, and sure to please.

GAUGE TO MEASURE WRAPS PER INCH

To make the most of a yarn substitution experience or identify the weight of a mystery skein, it is critical to accurately measure wraps per inch. The quickest way to do this is with a gauge demarked in the common yarn weights. For more accurate measurements, use a wraps per inch gauge. The two in my project bag double as comic relief when knit night gets a little too intense.

To figure out the weight of a yarn using a fixed-width gauge, lay the yarn into or onto the grooves of the gauge tool. Whichever groove approximates the yarn width best is the most likely weight of the yarn.

To compute the weight of a yarn using the wraps per inch method, gently wrap the yarn around the measurement marks on the tool, aligning the yarn wraps

Tools can be adorable and useful. Whether you are a cat or dog person, there is a wraps-per-inch tool that will make the task more fun. Shown here: Katrinkles' Cats per Inch and Dachshund Wraps per Inch tools are sure to make you smile. For quick access on my bag's handle, the brand's 2-inch-ruler keychain is smaller and always at the ready.

next to each other as you wrap it around the tool. When the yarn wraps cover the measurement surface, stop and count how many times the yarn was wrapped around one inch of the tool.

EMBROIDERY SCISSORS OR A SMALL POCKETKNIFE WITH A SCISSORS TOOL

A sharp pair of scissors is critical when making pom-poms and helpful for single snips. A small pair in your project bag won't take up much room and will be close at hand when needed. I keep one pair in my purse and one in my project bag. For frequent flyers, check with the airline and countries through which you plan to travel. Some get particular about what you can bring on board or into an airport. In a pinch, you can usually bring a nail clipper in your carry-on bag. Normally I advise purchasing the best tools you

My favorite scissors are a hand-forged pair given to me by a dear friend.

can afford to buy; the emergency yarn clipper is a rare exception. Cheaper is better, just in case you have to leave it behind at airport security.

NAIL FILE

There is nothing worse than discovering your wooden needle has a burr on it 10 miles offshore or 30,000 feet in the air. To keep your productivity up on the road, keep a disposable nail file in your project bag to sand off any burrs that develop on your wooden needles and to keep your fingernails smooth.

BAND-AIDS®

Because accidents happen, right? Sort of. A Band-Aid is helpful for covering up a paper cut and equally helpful when you need to secure the ends of your needles and project for transport. Unfurl half of the Band-Aid to expose the adhesive and then, holding the tips of two needles together, position the gauze over the needles and wrap the Band-Aid around and secure it to itself with the adhesive.

STITCH HOLDERS

Knit stitches are live stitches and therefore are subject to dropping off the needle and running back down through your project until they are bound off. To keep stitches orderly when working on a multipart project, it is useful to have stitch holders to which you can transition live stitches of one piece to use the needles on another piece. No need to get too fancy. When you need to hold just a few stitches, a locking stitch marker will work just fine. For more than five stitches, the use of a stitch holder or coil-less safety pin is recommended.

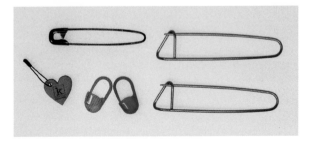

Clockwise from top left: Coil-less safety pin, pair of stitch holders, variety of locking stitch markers. The number of stitches to be held will determine the best tool for the job.

Pro Tip: A spare circular needle, two or three sizes smaller than the one used to knit the piece you need to set aside, can be used as a stitch holder. Use point protectors or rubber bands to slide over the points to hold the work on the circular needle.

RULER AND MEASURING TAPE

Measuring work in progress and final pieces is made easier by having the right tools close at hand. A small wooden ruler for short lengths and a measuring tape for larger pieces will help keep your work on target.

Pro Tip: If you don't have a ruler handy, US paper currency is 6 inches in length, so if you have a bill in your knitting bag for emergency coffee runs, you can use it to estimate length.

A ruler can double as a gauge tool and is helpful for measuring wraps per inch when the correct tool is not close enough at hand. A small ruler is particularly helpful for measuring at the beginning of a project where the work may be rolling. A ruler held flat on the work is easier to read than a measuring tape, as the latter is prone to undulating over the fabric and may result in inaccurate measurement.

Given how long it takes to make a garment by hand, it is important to consider the materials from which it is made. Color, texture, material, construction, and availability each play a role in the yarn selection process. In short, buy what suits the lifestyle of the person who will be wearing your knit piece of fiber art.

Pro Tip: The art of knitting is a tactile experience between the knitter, tools, and material used. To foster a better connection between you and your materials, wind your first skein of yarn by hand to get a truer sense of its ability to fulfill your vision for it. Listen to your thoughts as you manipulate it through your fingers. If it does not feel "right" now, it will not feel right as you cast on and bind off your project.

COLOR

Rather than bore you with the details of hue, intensity, contrast, and a bunch of other factoids about color, let me put it to you this way—use what you like and find inspiration from within your own life, not from some obscure color theory rule that may not suit your palette. For a basic overview of color theory, step out of the yarn section of your local bookstore and look for these instead—a collection of books telling the story of color through items that have retained their relevance through time. Bookmark the combinations you like and use them for inspiration when making yarn choices.

- *The Color Scheme Bible: Inspirational Palettes for Designing Home Interiors* by Anna Starmer
- *Pantone: The Twentieth Century in Color* by Leatrice Eiseman and Keith Recker
- *The V&A Book of Color in Design* by Tim Travis

Once you narrow down your palette, the yarn selection process can begin in earnest. Armed with your palette, whether in the form of a few bookmarks in one of the books above or another of your choosing, head to the local yarn store for guidance to find your yarn. If, like me, you don't have a local yarn store, there's always Zoom, FaceTime, or late-night, coffee-fueled trial-and-error online shopping. Before you head out, add a few pieces of equipment to your soon-to-be-filled project bag to aid in your selection process:

- Kaleidoscope or similar application on your smartphone
- Calculator, unless there's one on your phone
- Flashlight with an LED bulb, plain and simple
- Measuring device for wraps per inch

To better understand how a yarn may look when knitted, particularly a speckled yarn, use a kaleidoscope or kaleidoscope filter on your phone to look at a pixelated image of the yarn. This gives you a much better idea of how those fabulous little bits of color will work up together in a knitted or crocheted fabric. When selecting yarns of a single color or tonal colors with which to work, the kaleidoscope is equally helpful for discerning how the colors will work together as a knitted fabric, more accurately than simply placing the skeins next to each other on a table.

Once you make your color selections, a calculator is handy for double-checking your assumptions about the number of skeins of each color to buy and the total price of your project. Here's a simple equation to figure out how many skeins of a given yarn you'll need to buy if you are substituting one yarn for another. Assuming both are of similar construction, material, and weight, it's a quick calculation; just make sure you use the same units of measurement for each yarn.

$$\frac{\text{Number of yards or meters of yarn per skein of yarn specified in the pattern} \times \text{Number of skeins of yarn specified in the pattern}}{\text{Number of yards or meters of yarn per skein of yarn you want to use to make the pattern}}$$

= Number of skeins to purchase in the yarn you want to use

With the number of skeins figured out, you can multiply that by the cost per skein to calculate what the project will cost—helpful information to have when you are trying to choose between two different yarn solutions.

Yarn Weight Standards

The Craft Yarn Council (CYC) has put together helpful guidelines for yarn weight, needle sizes, and stitch counts, to aid you in selecting suitable yarn substitutions.

Standard Yarn Weight System
Categories of yarn, gauge ranges, and recommended needle and hook sizes

Yarn Weight Symbol & Category Names	0 LACE	1 SUPER FINE	2 FINE	3 LIGHT	4 MEDIUM	5 BULKY	6 SUPER BULKY	7 JUMBO
Type of Yarns in Category	Fingering, 10-Count Crochet Thread	Sock, Fingering, Baby	Sport, Baby	DK, Light Worsted	Worsted, Afghan, Aran	Chunky, Craft, Rug	Bulky, Roving	Jumbo, Roving
Knit Gauge Range in Stockinette Stitch to 4 inches*	33–40 sts**	27–32 sts	23–26 sts	21–24 st	16–20 sts	12–15 sts	7–11 sts	6 sts and fewer
Recommended Needle in Metric Size Range	1.5–2.25 mm	2.25–3.25 mm	3.25–3.75 mm	3.75–4.5 mm	4.5–5.5 mm	5.5–8 mm	8–12.75 mm	12.75 mm and larger
Recommended Needle in U.S. Size Range	000 to 1	1 to 3	3 to 5	5 to 7	7 to 9	9 to 11	11 to 17	17 and larger
Crochet Gauge Ranges in Single Crochet to 4 inches*	32–42 double crochets**	21–32 sts	16–20 sts	12–17 sts	11–14 sts	8–11 sts	7–9 sts	6 sts and fewer
Recommended Hook in Metric Size Range	Steel*** 1.6–1.4 mm Regular hook 2.25 mm	2.25–3.5 mm	3.5–4.5 mm	4.5–5.5 mm	5.5–6.5 mm	6.5–9 mm	9–15 mm	15 mm and larger
Recommended Hook in U.S. Size Range	Steel 6, 7, 8*** Regular hook B–1	B–1 to E–4	E–4 to 7	7 to I–9	I–9 to K–10½	K–10½ to M–13	M–13 to Q	Q and larger

* GUIDELINES ONLY: The above reflect the most commonly used gauges and needle or hook sizes for specific yarn categories.
** Lace weight yarns are usually knitted or crocheted on larger needles and hooks to create lacy, openwork patterns. Accordingly, a gauge range is difficult to determine. Always follow the gauge stated in your pattern.
*** Steel crochet hooks are sized differently from regular hooks—the higher the number, the smaller the hook, which is the reverse of regular hook sizing.

Source: Craft Yarn Council of America's **www.YarnStandards.com**

Information courtesy of the Craft Yarn Council.

As inviting as a yarn shop may be, it may not have sufficient light for you to comfortably make a yarn selection. While holding yarn near a window on a bright day is useful, if daylight is not available, a bright flashlight can help finalize your color selections. The flashlight is also useful if you are curious about how well a yarn may reflect the light or how the halo of a given yarn will catch the light. I prefer an LED flashlight to incandescent to get a true sense of the colors, as incandescent can cast a misleading yellow hue.

If your color adventures should take you to a new level of working with multiple yarns held together, a wooden ruler or similar measuring device will greatly improve the accuracy of your yarn substitution process. The wraps per inch of a yarn is a critical factor to consider when substituting one yarn for another. It is also helpful if you are trying to make your own special twisted cocktail of yarns to hold together. A tape measurer will not yield the same results as wrapping around something solid.

YARN SUBSTITUTIONS

What's a knitter to do when the yarn featured in a given pattern is no longer available, or it's not within the yarn budget? The options can be difficult to navigate, so let's start with a few steps to get headed in the right direction, and talk through some substitutions for the yarns featured in this book.

1. Shop your stash for the yarn in the pattern. You may surprise yourself and find just what you need for a swatch or the whole project. No stash? Ask knitting and crochet buddies; maybe someone has a little bit they can give you to create a swatch or can tell you what it is like to work with the yarn(s) in question. If you have even a few ounces of it, swatch with it and see how the yarn performs, regardless of the color you have—the swatch won't care if it's done in the precise shade envisioned for the pattern itself. Use this as the base of any comparative analysis you may do to find a substitute yarn.

2. Ask an expert. Plain and simple: just ask. Discuss the pattern with your local yarn store proprietor and get his/her opinion regarding a good substitute.

Pro Tip: Many yarn companies send sample skeins to local yarn stores for promotional purposes. Even if the local yarn store does not carry the yarn needed, it doesn't hurt to ask if there is a promotional skein in the shop stash from which you could make a swatch.

   If you don't have a local yarn store, ask the designer or yarn company directly via email or via their official website.

Pro Tip: Most designers and yarn companies have a social media following on Instagram or via a Facebook group. Search therein for yarn substitutions.

3. Read the pattern notes and any designer notes pertaining to the yarn(s) used. Consider the characteristics of the original yarn used in the pattern when choosing a substitute yarn. Some designers, like me, will include specific characteristics of a given yarn that played into the yarn selection for a particular collection. See, for example, my notes on Universal Yarn Colorburst. I chose it for this book because it is available in a wide range of colorways; the color runs within the skein are very long, making for great stripes and no ends to weave in to create the gentle undulating stripes; and the yarn has a bit of a halo on it, which helps it retain its shape and not droop as some superwash wools are prone to doing over time.

4. Refer to Yarnsub.com, my favorite source of alternative yarn ideas. Many yarns that are commercially manufactured and available internationally are listed in the yarnsub.com database. You may not find that delicious hand-dyed yarn from the local farmers market that you forgot to buy after you picked out your potatoes, but you likely can find a good substitute for it if you search on yarn attributes such as composition and weight.

5. Consider what "it" is you love about the pattern. Is it the yarn? The drape? The overall proportions of the pattern? The answer to this will determine the path of your yarn substitution.

a. If it's the yarn: Consider the qualities of the yarn that drew you to it: texture of the fibers, dye method, colors, number of plies, care, composition, and construction. Check through your yarn stash for yarn with similar characteristics and swatch with it. If you don't have anything on hand, work with your local yarn store to find the perfect fiber to work the first swatch, and discuss the feasibility of using that fiber for the entire project.

b. If it's the drape: Review the pattern stitch and pattern notes. Is it the stitch that is creating the drape, or the yarn itself? The same stitch pattern executed in different yarns will yield different results. Take the case of my two cabled poncho designs, the Pacific Poncho and the Atlantic Poncho (pages 103 and 98). Both are the same weight yarn and same pattern stitch. The drape of the #3/DK-weight Blue Heron Rayon Metallic is very different than that of the #3/DK-weight hand-dyed superwash wool from Cozy Color Works. When worn, the former will flow like a silken layer for a shimmering effect as you breeze through your day regardless of the temperature, and the latter will keep you warm on a breezy day.

c. If it's the pattern: Research the yarn used and find a substitute with similar qualities to ensure a good outcome from the substitute yarn. If there is colorwork in a pattern, think about the pattern itself and the yarn used by the designer versus the yarn you may envision using. The strength of a colorwork pattern is relative to the composition and contrast of the individual yarns, stitch work in the pattern, and colors. In short, different yarns will produce different results.

6. Never underestimate the power of holding multiple strands together and mixing weights to get the desired outcome, unless the pattern incorporates complicated lacework or openwork. For lacework and openwork it is best to use a yarn of similar weight and construction to that of the pattern, as both rely heavily upon the interplay of stitch pattern and the yarn itself.

To figure out the ideal number of strands to hold together for your first swatch, you will need to know the number of wraps per inch for each yarn you want to use, and the wraps per inch of the yarn used in the pattern. Use as many strands of your preferred yarn as needed to approximate the number of wraps per inch of the yarn in the pattern to make your first gauge swatch. This is where the yarn gauge tools discussed earlier are very useful.

For example, if the pattern calls for 1,000 yards of #3/DK-weight yarn measuring 13 wraps per inch, and you find lace weight you'd prefer to use, which measures 38 wraps per inch, divide the wraps per inch of the yarn you have by the wraps per inch of the yarn in the pattern to find the number of strands you need; 38/13 = 2.9. Ideally, to get 13 wraps per inch from the 38 wraps per inch lace-weight yarn, 2.9 strands held together will yield a similar weight yarn. Rounding this up to three strands is the starting point of your yarn substitution journey and the number of strands to use for your first swatch. If your gauge swatch is too big, use the same needle and try two strands. If the gauge is still not right, try a different needle.

Depending on the pattern, most of the time the stitch count is more important than the row count, so if after making three swatches with three different needles and strand combinations I find that I am still not getting the Holy Grail of gauge stitch and row count, I tend to go with the combination of yarn and needle that gets me closest to the desired stitch gauge.

Pro Tip: When your knitted swatch is really close to your target gauge yet not quite correct, make another swatch using another set of needles of the same size made from a different material or with a different tip.

7. The total yardage required to complete a project is a factor of the number of strands held together. Going back to our example of a pattern that specifies 1,000 yards of #3/DK-weight yarn, if the three strands of lace weight held together produce the desired gauge, you will need three times as much yarn to complete the project: 3 × 1,000 = 3,000.

8. After completing the last of the swatches and before diving into the project, wash the winning swatch if it's washable and block it to see what the "finished hand" will be like. If the yarn is not washable, use a little steam to relax the fibers and block them; see "Blocking" on page 31 for more information.

Pro Tip: When using a superwash wool, or bamboo, silk, or any fiber lacking the memory of wool, after measuring the swatch let it hang for a few days to see how it may grow over time. I made the mistake of skipping this last step once. I substituted one yarn for another, got the correct gauge, blocked it to the correct dimensions, and the resulting sweater was a disaster because I did not realize the superwash wool I was substituting for the merino wool was unable to hold the stitch pattern and drooped like a weeping willow when worn.

With all this said, what follows are my ideas in case you need to find substitutes for the yarns used in this collection.

Blue Heron
Rayon Metallic
Used for: Pacific Poncho (page 103), Santa Monica Shell (page 137)
Blue Heron Rayon Metallic has no easy substitute. It is a unique #3/DK-weight, 85% rayon/15% metallic blend. The 15% metallic content is in the form of fine metallic threads twisted along with the eight plies of rayon throughout to give it a fine luster. Most of the colors are available with any one of three metallic

threads—gold, silver, and copper—to provide a wider selection of options for your projects. Each skein of yarn is hand painted in Delaware. The yarn base is sourced domestically, making this a 100% USA-made product. The skeins are a generous 550 yd/502 m per 8 oz/227 g featuring fields of color ranging from tonal of a single color to variegated colorways. The yarn is machine washable and dries quickly, which makes it a good option for those who favor caring for their knitwear at home rather than sending it out.

When looking for a substitute, consider the drape of your finished garment. Choose yarn of similar weight with a high bamboo/rayon or silk content to provide a similar tactile experience. Universal Yarn Wool Pop has a similar hand to Rayon Metallic and will perform well over time if used in lieu of Rayon Metallic. The multiple fibers in Wool Pop—50% bamboo/35% superwash wool/15% polyamide—give it a lovely sheen to capture the light as it reflects off the knitted fabric. The tonal nature of Wool Pop is derived from the way in which each material takes the dye, while the tonal relationships in Rayon Metallic are derived from the hand-painting process and will present differently.

Universal Yarn Wool Pop (used in these two swatches) has a similar hand to that of Blue Heron Rayon Metallic (balled). Both are washable and provide a unique bespoke elegance in the way they catch the light.

At 284 yd/260 m per 3.5 oz/100 g skein Wool Pop (bottom) is a close match to the weight and density of Rayon Metallic (top). It is not spun quite as tightly as Rayon Metallic and presents as a bit thicker when knit, but will block to similar dimensions. When knit up, you can see the underlying tonal relationship between swatches: the hand-painted shades of rust in the Blue Heron Rayon Metallic and its slight shimmer on the top versus the single-color presentation of the Wool Pop shown below it in the gauge tool.

Another option to add a metallic finish to a non-metallic comparable yarn is to hold a thin metallic strand with your substitute yarn. Metalika from Bergère de France is available in gold, silver, white, black, and copper to complement your yarn selection.

Cozy Color Works

Cozy Color Works yarns are dyed by hand in small lots by Sandy Anderson at her studio in New Jersey. It is available online directly from the website (https://www.cozycolorworks.com/) and from a select group of retailers with online stores, including Knit in Roslyn, New York (https://www.knitlongisland.com). This line was chosen for the treatment of color and range of weights in which the yarn is available. The gentle undulating tones of the Cozy Color Works line provide visual interest as they are knit and worn. Each tonal color in the line has at least one complementary partner—whether another tonal or a speckled yarn—which makes color selections less stressful. For instance, the navy used in the Newport Clambake Poncho (page 108) is brought to life by the coordinated blues in the Deep Blue Sea speckled yarn with which it is paired.

Shown here is the interplay between English Garden Worsted and Spruce Bulky. Regardless of the weights, Cozy Color Works yarns are dyed to make your color selections less stressful.

Cozy Color Works takes great care to maintain the tonal relationships of their yarns across multiple weights as shown here in the Nantucket Tradewinds Hat (page 67) and Coronado Cowl (page 59), knit in #4/worsted-weight and #1/fingering-weight yarn respectively.

Substitutions for Cozy Color Works will not have the same color characteristics, as every independent dyer uses their own proprietary formulation and methods to create their artisanal yarns. When considering alternatives, it is important to think through the similarities and the differences between the hand-dyed artisanal yarns herein and a substitute product.

Fingering

Used for: Coronado Sands Cowl (page 59), Newport Clambake Poncho (page 108)

Cozy Color Works Fingering yarn is a #1/super-fine-weight, two-ply, superwash merino wool with a smooth texture, consistently dyed throughout the skein in a wide range of tonal and speckled colorways from which to make your selections. The length of each color in a speckled skein is short in order to produce a brief pop of color as it is worked and provide a bit of visual interest. Each skein is approximately 550 yd/503 m per 3.5 oz/100 g skein.

Commercially milled and dyed alternative yarns abound in #1/super-fine-weight yarn. When considering alternatives in this weight class, don't fall into the trap of thinking #1/sock-weight yarn is the same as #1/fingering-weight yarn. They are similar in yardage/meterage per ounce/gram and wraps per inch; however, sock yarn typically has nylon spun into it and tends to be more tightly spun to help it stand up to the wear and tear a sock takes over the course of its life. In addition to the construction and materials, the color runs in sock yarn tend to be optimized for knitting it into its intended shape—a sock. Notice how the Darn Good Yarn's Indigo Quail Alanya Sock Yarn used on the Intercoastal Sunrise Poncho (page 114) presents as thin stripes, while the hand-dyed yarn from Cozy Color Works (Newport Clambake Poncho, page 108) presents as a field of undulating navy tonals with stripes added, using a speckled yarn from their collection. Although both are washable and the yarns are of similar weight, Darn Good Yarn Indigo Quail Alanya Sock Yarn knits into a more sturdy-feeling finished fabric because the yarn is more tightly spun and contains nylon.

Yarn Bee Tonals, available at Hobby Lobby, provide a similar hand to Cozy Color Works. It is hand dyed, albeit commercially in large batches. When purchasing Yarn Bee, be mindful of the batches and check even within the same dye lots for color consistency. At 420 yd/384 m per 3.5 oz/100 g skein, it is more dense than Cozy Color Works Fingering. The speckled yarns currently available have color runs that will yield more stitches per color and present as bigger spots of color per inch, compared to the delicate dots of Cozy Color Works. For a bit of additional flair, Yarn Bee also offers a version of this weight with metallic bits throughout.

The delicate interplay of artfully applied dyes makes the Cozy Color Works yarn unique, evoking an emotion reminiscent of a delicate impressionist painting. Shown here is Long Island Sound.

Yarn Bee Tonals shown in November Sky with metallic thread throughout. Note the difference in the length of each color run of Yarn Bee November Sky versus Cozy Color Works Long Island Sound in the previous photo.

For a sumptuous alternative to wool, try Universal Yarn Fibra Natura Cashmere Lusso. Available in 246 yd/225 m per 1.75 oz/50 g cakes, it is similar in weight to Cozy Color Works Fingering. Cashmere Lusso is an ecological option, artfully blended by layering virgin cashmere and cashmere sourced from sweaters of similar tones to create a delightfully decadent fiber available in a range of colors, including one as rich and relaxing as the sands on the beach in San Diego—which inspired the Coronado Sands Cowl (page 59). To show you how beautifully Cashmere Lusso works with Cozy Color Works, the cowl was worked up in both yarns, sand and sea versions.

For a warmer-weather luxury alternative, Universal Yarn Fibra Natura Ravello, available in 207 yd/190 m per 1.75 oz/50 g cakes, offers the luxury of 9% recycled cashmere spun with 75% cotton and 16% extra-fine merino wool in a select group of colors. The individual fibers take the dye in slightly different ways to create a tonal consistency throughout the entire project, as shown in the Nauset Beach Bandana (page 73). The proportions of the fibers give this yarn the advantage of remaining comfortable in a warmer climate while showing off your stitch work. By weight and yardage, it is a bit lighter than Cozy Color Works Fingering and can be worked at the same gauge.

DK

Used for: Atlantic Poncho (page 98)
Cozy Color Works DK is a smooth, 4-ply, superwash merino sold in 275 yd/251 m per 3.5 oz/100 g skeins. This yarn was selected for this collection for its calm tonal relationships within each skein and across the weights in which it is available. The gentle undulation of colors in the lighter blues and more vibrant changes between skeins of darker/deeper colors like navy blue are reminiscent of the colors one finds at the water's edge as the noon sun dances across the bay. Even the names evoke a sense of calm and happiness: English Garden, Long Island Sound, and Sea Spray, to name a few.

The gauge of Cozy Color Works DK is closely aligned to that of Universal Yarn Deluxe DK Superwash.

On a field of Cozy Color Works are three of the swatches done in Universal Yarn #3/DK-weight yarns to spark the imagination and show some of the differences when substituting yarns. Each worked up to the same gauge prior to blocking, before taking this picture. After blocking, slight differences in gauge became apparent. Each one has its own personality and final post-blocking gauge: the darker Colorburst; the royal blue Deluxe DK Superwash; and in the center, the softest of the three, Dona, in a light cornflower blue shade.

Yarn Bee Hand-Dyed Vivid #3 comes in a wide range of colors and—like its lighter #1 weight partner—it has tonal qualities similar to those of an artisanal small-batch hand-dyed yarn. At 215 yd/196 m per 3.5 oz/100 g skein, it is a bit heavier and more dense than Cozy Color Works. It is a smooth two-ply yarn.

Universal Yarn Fibra Natura Dona is a commercially dyed yarn of 100% extra-fine merino available in 126 yd/115 m per 1.75 oz/50 g cakes. It is a fine Italian-style merino with an exceptionally light hand. Dona is available in a wide range of colors. While the yarns are not tonal, the hand is similar to that of the Cozy Color Works DK when knit, so if the desired result is for a single color without tonal variation, this is an excellent option. For an example of how it knits up, take a look at the Cold Spring Harbor Hooded Shawl (page 87), where it was used as the main color. For those who may find comfort in the reduced environmental impact of a given fiber, Dona is Oeko-Tex 100 Product Class 1 certified. (For additional information on Oeko-Tex certification, see https://www.oeko-tex.com/.)

For a budget-friendly #3/DK-weight alternative, consider Universal Yarn Deluxe DK Superwash. It is 100% wool and available in a wide range of colors. At 284 yd/259 m per 3.5 oz/100 g ball it is a very close match in terms of weight versus meterage to Cozy Color Works DK.

Worsted
Used for: Nantucket Tradewinds Hat (page 67), Orchids in Martello Tower Shawl (page 78)
Cozy Color Works Worsted is a four-ply, smooth texture, 100% superwash merino wool available in 200 yd/183 m per 3.5 oz/100 g skeins. This yarn was chosen for two of the Nantucket Tradewinds Hats (page 67) in this collection because of the way the tonal yarn catches the color and the four-ply construction complements the texture of the hats. This yarn in English Garden, a speckled version, is featured in the Orchids in Martello Tower Shawl (page 78), where the colors highlight each other as they grace the trellis-like stitch.

For a commercially dyed option, Universal Yarn Deluxe Worsted Wool and Deluxe Worsted Superwash are both good alternatives. They are available in 220 yd/200 m per 3.5 oz/100 g skeins, a close match to Cozy Color Works Worsted. For those who may prefer a tweedy look, Deluxe Worsted Superwash has a complementary selection of tweed options available. The most appealing aspect of the Universal Yarn Superwash line is how beautifully it mimics its non-superwash cousin. Unlike a lot of commercially manufactured superwash yarns that droop and drip when worn, the Universal Yarn Deluxe Superwash line does not; it retains its shape nicely throughout the day and wash after wash.

For a commercially dyed option with similar washability and texture in a non-animal fiber, try Lion Brand Heartland. It is 100% acrylic and available in a range of solid colors and tweed colorways. The yarn has a similar hand, and the four-ply construction makes textured work pop. The yarn comes in balls of 251 yd/230 m per 5 oz/142 g. It is denser than Cozy Color Works and will therefore make a thicker fabric, so swatch carefully.

I Love This Yarn, a 100% acrylic alternative, provides a good budget yarn for larger projects and for the knitter who may prefer a true traditional variegated yarn over the more modern, subtle speckled, tonal, and barber-pole yarns. For a bit of additional flash, I Love This Yarn is also available in a limited number of colors with a metallic ply spun into it, not unlike the effect of the same in the lighter-weight Yarn Bee Authentic Hand-Dyed Luxe. At 252 yd/230 m per 5 oz/142 g, it is the most budget-friendly option.

Bulky
Used for: San Francisco Cabled Cowl (page 49), Montauk Waves Headband/Cowl (page 53)
There is something immensely satisfying about finishing a project quickly in a sumptuous yarn. At 100 yd/92 m per 3.5 oz/100 g skein, Cozy Color Works Bulky is just the yarn for the task. Hand dyed in the same color palette as the rest of the line, the #5/bulky-weight yarn is very soft and has a smooth

texture to hold a cable well, thus the reason I chose to use it for the San Francisco Cabled Cowl (page 49) and the Montauk Waves Headband/Cowl (page 53).

Other indie hand-dyed options in this weight class are difficult to find because #5/bulky-weight yarn takes quite a bit more dye to saturate the fibers than lighter yarns. When looking for an alternative, always unfurl the skein to make sure the dye has taken consistently throughout the skein, and buy enough to complete the project you have in mind so as not to be disappointed with your results. If more than one skein is used, it is best to use two skeins at a time, alternating every round or every two rows.

Universal Yarn Deluxe Bulky Superwash is a good alternative to Cozy Color Works, at 106 yd/97 m per 3.5 oz/100 g cake. Like the rest of the Universal Yarn Deluxe Superwash line, it is available in a range of colors, has a pleasant twist, and stands up to multiple trips through the washing machine. For a side-by-side single project comparison, look at the San Francisco Cabled Cowl (page 49).

Pro Tip: When choosing #5/bulky-weight yarn, remember to check the twist and number of plies—it can make a big difference. Too few plies and the yarn will not hold a textured stitch. A #5/bulky-weight single ply should be avoided, as it tends to fall apart unless paired with other weight fibers to hold it together.

Darn Good Yarn

The selection of hand dyed and ethically sourced products on the Darn Good Yarn website are a wonderful reminder that with the right leadership, there are ways for a company to foster economic development and be fashionable at the same time. The two yarns in the Darn Good Yarn line that are used in this book were chosen for their drape and colorways. Both are available from their website, http://www.darngoodyarn.com. Darn Good Yarn is not sold in stores.

Darn Good Yarn (DGY) was started in 2008 by Nicole Snow, and is built on a foundation of love, hard work, and creativity. DGY has a commitment to flipping the script on fast fashion. With a focus on

Superwash wool is a good option for garments that may be subject to the occasional lipstick or makeup contact, which makes it perfect for the San Francisco Cabled Cowl (page 49).

At right: The tonal relationships of Cozy Color Works Bulky Weight yarn (top) present a different look than the commercially dyed Universal Yarn Deluxe Bulky Superwash (bottom) at a similar gauge.

providing safe employment opportunities and fair pay for artisans at co-ops in India, DGY is on a mission to reduce textile waste. Silk and sari materials that were destined to end up in landfills are instead recycled into yarn, crafting supplies, and apparel.

Lace Weight Silk
Used for: East Bay Coastline Shawl (page 82)
Lace Weight Silk is a single-ply, 100% recycled silk hand-dyed yarn. At 300 yd/275 m per 1.75 oz/50 g skein, a similar #1 weight yarn is difficult to find. Substitutions should be carefully considered in terms of the number of plies and yarn texture. The silk fibers of Lace Weight Silk are smooth and consistent with minor variations throughout the skein to catch the light as you wear it. Mondal, bamboo, and cashmere—depending upon the yarn construction—are suitable substitute fibers.

Universal Yarn Magnolia, available in single colors, is more dense than Lace Weight Silk at 361 yd/330 m per 3.5 oz/100 g skein, and will produce a fabric of similar hand as a substitute for Lace Weight Silk when making the East Bay Coastline Shawl (page 82). For a variegated option, Universal Yarn Bamboo Sock Pop is a 100% wool-free option. Don't let the middle name, "Sock," fool you into thinking it's rough; the cotton and bamboo make up a hefty 92% of the composition to keep it soft and perfect for wearing next to the skin. It comes in solid and variegated colorways to enliven your knitting as you effortlessly stitch up your own East Bay Coastline Shawl. If the precise gauge of the shawl is not relevant to you, try making one out of Blue Heron Rayon Metallic.

Indigo Quail Alanya Sock Yarn
Used for: Intracoastal Sunrise Poncho (page 114)
Alanya Sock is a self-striping, #1/super-fine-weight yarn from the Indigo Quail line available exclusively from Darn Good Yarn. Sold in pairs of 130 yd/119 m per 1 oz/30 g cakes, it is hand dyed in small batches wherein the colors are matched throughout the skeins to present even color distribution straight off the cake and into your work, forming thin sophisticated stripes as shown in the Intercoastal Sunrise Poncho (page 114). A suitable substitute for similar results would be another hand-dyed, self-striping sock yarn or—for a speckled alternative—try Universal Yarn Bamboo Pop Sock. Bamboo Pop Sock's color repeats will create more of a stippled look than the striped effect of the Alanya, as it knits into a more subtle field and transitions from color to color. For a budget alternative, try Patons Kroy. Kroy has a more definitive break between colors and while it works up at a similar gauge, it has shorter runs of color that will present as smaller stripes.

Toby Roxane Designs
Toby Roxane Barna is the artist behind the dye pots at Toby Roxane Designs, nestled in the heart of the Hudson Valley not far from Rhinebeck, New York. Her line is available at a select number of retail outlets as well as via her website, http://tobyroxanedesigns.com.

Toby is an independent knitwear designer and dyer of luxury yarns. She began her design career in 2012, and since then has released over 90 patterns and self-published three books. She is the author of *Design Doubles* (Stackpole Books, 2018) and *Easy Knits for Beautiful Yarns* (Stackpole Books, 2021); her designs have been featured in publications such as Knitty.com, *Knitting Traditions*, and *I Like Knitting*; and she has contributed patterns to several Interweave compilations.

Toby fell in love with dyeing in 2015, and she now sells her yarn at festivals, trunk shows, and yarn shops. She especially enjoys being able to design patterns specifically for her yarn, and vice versa.

Beautilitarian DK
Used for: Nantucket Storm Cocoon (page 125)
The first time I saw Toby's Beautilitarian DK, I knew it had to be included in a coastal collection. The

colorway I chose, Summer Storm, is absolutely that of the summer storm as the ocean churns, trees blow along the shoreline, and lightning dances briefly across the sky. Dyed in small batches, this smooth #3/DK-weight, four-ply yarn presents with equally impressive results in both knit and crocheted fabrics. Paired in this collection with a simple textured knit fabric, it provides the beginner knitter with a visual treat as each stitch is worked.

For commercially dyed yarn alternatives, consider the same as those recommended for use with the Cozy Color Works DK yarns (page 16). Beautilitarian DK is a little denser than Cozy Color Works with 250 yd/229 m per 3.5 oz/100 g skein.

Pascuali

Most American consumers have not had the pleasure of working with Pascuali's line. It is available at a select number of retailers in North America and online at https://www.pascuali.de/en. The company is committed to ethical manufacture and sourcing of its raw material. The company takes its environmental impact seriously from start to finish; they even ship their yarn in brown paper bags rather than plastic.

Balayage
Used for: Oyster Bay Skirt (page 144)
Balayage is a blend of 80% alpaca and 20% organic extra-fine merino wool spun and dyed in Peru to create a fine yarn suitable for garments worn next to the skin. Available in 190 yd/175 m per 1.75 oz/50 g cakes, the alpaca provides a warm lightweight halo effect while the wool content helps the alpaca retain its shape, making it the perfect yarn for a skirt like the Oyster Bay Skirt (page 144). For a 100% superwash extra-fine merino option, Universal Yarn Fibra Natura Donnina will produce similar results at a similar meterage-to-weight ratio of 180 yd/165 m per 1.75 oz/50 g cake.

Alpaca Royal
Used for: St. Michaels Fog Sweater (page 130)
Alpaca Royal, featured in the St. Michaels Fog Sweater, is a three-ply, #1/fingering-weight yarn composed of 80% alpaca royal and 20% baby alpaca made in Peru, available in a 145 yd/133 m per 0.88 oz/25 g cake. The colors available are derived from the natural colors of the fibers from which it is spun. The yarn itself is exceptionally soft, and the three plies twisted together hold shape well without the droop

The warmth of alpaca and the memory of wool make Pascuali Balayage the perfect yarn for the Oyster Bay Skirt.

one might expect from alpaca. The yarn has a delicate halo and, when doubled, presents at a pleasant-to-work gauge similar to that of a #3/DK-weight yarn. The yarn is held double throughout the St. Michaels Fog Sweater project, so if Alpaca Royal is not available, a #3/DK-weight yarn may be substituted.

Substitutes for Alpaca Royal depend on the desired results and preference for or against holding a yarn double throughout a project. I find holding a yarn doubled presents me with additional options. By holding two strands of a yarn like alpaca or silk together, the resulting fabric has a light hand capable of keeping the wearer warmer than a similar garment knit out of a thicker yarn. The ability of alpaca to trap the warm air next to the body makes this a good yarn for layered knits, particularly favorable for under a sports jacket or other lightweight outer layer when the man lucky enough to have this knit sweater in his closet needs just a bit more warmth than a heavy coat and wants to wear something more presentable than a hoodie or sweatshirt.

Organic Cashmere Lace, also from Pascuali, is similar to Alpaca Royal and comes in a wider range of colors. Organic Cashmere Lace is lighter at 185 yd/170 m per 0.88 oz/25 g cake. If you prefer to buy an alternate yarn and not hold it doubled throughout, Universal

Yarn Fibra Natura Dona is an excellent machine-washable option. If bespoke sophistication is desired, Universal Yarn Fibra Natura Cashmere Lusso may be held doubled to produce a similar fabric.

Saffira

Used for: Key West Shrimper Hat (page 63)
With four plies of ultrafine merino and mulberry silk tightly spun and dyed in Italy, Saffira knows how to hold a stitch. It is the perfect balance of warmth and breathability on cold mornings in warm climates or cold winter days in the frozen north. This is my go-to yarn for men's hats and accessories because it is not only warm, it is also hand or delicate cycle machine washable and highly elastic to hold on when the winter wind howls. Inspired by the sea, the colorways of Saffira catch the light in the silk fibers and reflect it back with a sophistication I have not found in other yarns. Even the darkest of blues has a vibrancy to it. The 218 yd/200 m per 1.75 oz/50 g cakes are also available undyed.

If a substitute is desired, Universal Yarn Wool Pop is a good option. The combination of bamboo, wool, and polyamide in Wool Pop provides a similar sheen to silk as the fibers take the dye in slightly different tones, creating a varied surface across which the light can play. The characteristics of both yarns are

Pascuali Alpaca Royal is exceptionally soft and warm, perfect for the St. Michaels Fog Sweater.

Saffira captures and reflects light beautifully due to the silk content, while the merino wool helps it hold a great stitch.

different, so make sure you swatch when substituting, adding, or decreasing the number of stitches if necessary to create the perfect fit.

Universal Yarn

For more than 15 years, Universal Yarn has been offering high-quality yarns produced with care in a broad range of fiber content, colors, and beautiful patterns to support each yarn, so while you browse, you can look at how each yarn works up and perhaps pick out a few additional projects. Fair warning: a trip to the Universal Yarn website may be a long one. In addition to the yarns they offer, the company also has a curated collection of handcrafted accessories to meet every crafting need. Universal Yarn believes that crafting is universal, and strives to inspire knitters, crocheters, and all fiber artists while providing exceptional customer service. Widely distributed in North America, Universal Yarn fibers were used extensively in this collection. The line offers an enticing number of options for texture, composition, and color across yarn weights. If Universal Yarn is not available at your local yarn store, the colorway you need may be available on the website, http://universalyarn.com.

Wool Pop
Used for: Delaware River Mitts (page 40)
Wool Pop is a versatile multi-season yarn. It is 50% bamboo, 35% superwash wool, and 15% polyamide blended together to create a soft, washable yarn that performs well in a variety of projects. The blending of wool and bamboo gives the yarn a slight sheen, and because the fibers take the dye in slightly different ways, the yarn has an additional layer of visual interest as the tonal relationships between each fiber work together to present as a whole. It is a staple in my studio for its soft hand, ability to dance in the light, and the wide range of colors in which it is available. The yarn works up at a similar gauge to its bamboo and cotton partner, Bamboo Pop, holds textured stitches nicely, and stands up to repeated

The wide range of colors, from brilliant and saturated to calm and cool, in which Wool Pop is available makes it a solid staple in your collection.

washing—critical characteristics for any yarn destined to become an accessory or wardrobe staple. Wool Pop is a suitable substitute for Blue Heron Rayon Metallic when making the Pacific Poncho, as both will work up at a similar gauge with a similar hand. If a lighter-weight fabric is desired when making the Delaware River Mitts, Bamboo Pop would work as a suitable substitute for Wool Pop.

Fibra Natura Cashmere Lusso
Used for: Coronado Sands Cowl (page 59)
Cashmere Lusso is a blend of 50% virgin cashmere and 50% recycled cashmere sourced from sweaters of similar color tones. The resulting fiber, spun in Italy, is exceptionally soft and a treat to wear next to the skin. Available in a range of sophisticated colors, Cashmere Lusso offers elegance with an uncanny ability to show off texture. If a substitute is preferred for warmer weather wear, Ravello, also from Universal Yarn Fibra Natura, works up at a similar gauge and comes in a range of colors. For a budget-friendly alternative, Donnina is a 100% extra-fine merino wool, machine-washable option.

Fibra Natura Ravello
Used for: Nauset Beach Bandana (page 73)
The recycled cashmere fibers combine effortlessly into the mix of cotton and extra-fine merino to make Universal Yarn Fibra Natura Ravello soft and whisper thin as a layer to wear next to the skin. The

75% cotton makes Ravello a great option for warmer climates, while the 9% recycled cashmere and 16% extra-fine merino help the yarn stay aligned for good stitch definition. Each of the fibers in Ravello takes the dye in a slightly different way, making it a fascinating blend of color as it is worked. The tonal relationships between the fibers create a consistent field of color with a faint halo. Suitable alternatives to Ravello include the warmer Cashmere Lusso or Donnina.

Ravello was used for the Nauset Beach Bandana (page 73) in this book. Since it's a bandana, not a precisely fitted garment, you may also want to consider two more yarns to make the Nauset Beach Bandana your own: Universal Yarn Wool Pop or Magnolia. Wool Pop's combination of bamboo, wool, and polyamide creates a similar hand to Ravello at a heavier gauge. Universal Yarn Magnolia, a 95% modal and 5% cashmere blend, produces a subtle silken fabric available in a full range of cheerful colors. Two skeins of either make a lovely version of the same design at a slightly larger gauge.

Fibra Natura Dona

Used for: Cold Spring Harbor Hooded Shawl (page 87)
Six tightly wound plies of two plies each in 100% superwash extra-fine merino give Universal Yarn Fibra Natura Dona a spring to its step and the ability to hold your textured stitches beautifully (it is also Oeko-Tex certified). It was chosen for this collection to provide the perfect balance of twist needed to make a comfortable but not-too-snug hood for the Cold Spring Harbor Hooded Shawl (page 87) while providing the washability needed for a go-to staple in your wardrobe. The wide selection of Dona colors go well with the equally washable and wearable Colorburst that they were paired with in the hooded shawl. When choosing a substitute for this particular project, consider the compatibility of both yarns in your selection process.

Universal Yarn Deluxe DK Superwash is a good substitute for Dona. It knits up at the same gauge, and while it is not quite as tightly spun, its four-ply 100% superwash wool makes it a more budget-friendly choice than Dona. It too pairs well with Colorburst. If an acrylic yarn is desired, Universal Yarn Uptown DK is a good option. For a vegan option, consider Universal Yarn Cotton Supreme DK; the twist is good, it comes in "grown-up" colors, and it holds up well wash after wash.

Pro Tip: When looking for options at the same gauge for a finished garment, always make your final choices based on your budget and desired finished garment; one may be more suitable than the other.

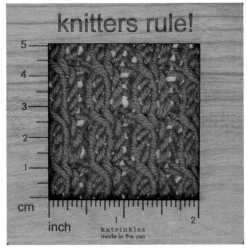

While Deluxe DK Superwash (left) and Dona (right) both work up at a similar gauge, Dona has a lighter hand due to its superfine merino content and the way in which the yarn is plied.

Colorburst

Used for: Cold Spring Harbor Hooded Shawl (page 87), Ocean Beach Sunset Shawl/Poncho (page 93), Seven Mile Bridge Poncho (page 118)

Colorburst is a unique single-ply yarn with long runs of color that flow effortlessly throughout each 660 yd/600 m per 7 oz/200 g ball. The self-striping nature of this yarn presents well on an adult-sized garment, as seen on the front of the Seven Mile Bridge Poncho (page 118). The high percentage of wool in this yarn, 65% superwash fine merino, provides it with the soft hand and stability a knitter desires while the 35% acrylic provides the owner of the finished object with an easy-to-care-for fabric.

Shown here in a preliminary set of swatches for the Seven Mile Bridge Poncho, the two plies of Cobblestone 100% superwash merino present a more marbled look when paired with the Deluxe Worsted Superwash chosen for the back.

Cobblestone, in the smaller "knitters rule!" gauge tool, and Colorburst, in the background and in the larger "knitters rule!" gauge tool, placed side by side to show how the two complement each other in the same stitch.

For those who are allergic to wool or prefer not to use it, Red Heart Unforgettable is a self-striping 100% acrylic alternative. Yarn Bee Chloe, 70% wool/30% viscose, is a heavier alternative at 270 yd/247 m per 3.5 oz/100 g that will produce similar results at a slightly different gauge, with thinner stripes or pooling depending on the size of the finished garment.

For additional visual interest or for those who prefer not to use acrylic yarn, Universal Yarn Fibra Natura Cobblestone is a barber-poled, two-ply 100% superwash merino wool. Cobblestone will provide similar gauge results to Colorburst with a marbled pattern and a twist—literally. It is slightly heavier than Colorburst at 612 yd/560 m per 7 oz/200 g ball and complements the Deluxe Superwash line well.

Deluxe DK Superwash

Used for: Ocean Beach Sunset Shawl/Poncho (page 93)

Universal Yarn Deluxe DK Superwash is a 100% superwash wool available in a range of solid and tweed colors. Together this group provides a wide range of colorwork options. As with the others in this line it too is Oeko-Tex Standard 100 Product Class 1 certified.

Universal Yarn Uptown DK is a 100% acrylic yarn perfect for those who prefer or require a non-animal fiber. Gentle on the earth, Uptown DK is also Oeko-Tex Standard 100 Product Class 1 certified. It will work up at the same gauge and similar hand to Deluxe DK Superwash.

Deluxe Worsted and Deluxe Worsted Superwash

Used for: Seven Mile Bridge Poncho (page 118), Oyster Creek Mitts (page 45), Nantucket Tradewinds Hat (page 67)

The #4/worsted-weight yarns in the Universal Yarn family work very well together. Without checking the label, it is nearly impossible to discern the difference between the Deluxe Worsted Superwash and Deluxe Worsted, which makes them excellent substitutes for each other. For frequently used items requiring regular washings—like mitts worn on public transportation—my go-to is the Deluxe Worsted Superwash. It holds texture well and does not droop like lesser superwash yarns from other companies. It is a true #4/worsted-weight like its traditional wool cousin, Deluxe Worsted.

Universal Yarn Uptown Worsted, like its #3/DK-weight cousin, is a 100% acrylic yarn that performs in a similar fashion to the Cozy Color Works Worsted and Universal Yarn Deluxe Worsted. Available in over 50 colors, there's likely an option available to suit your project goals. As with the Uptown DK, it too meets the Oeko-Tex standards and complements its wool cousins in the Universal Yarn Deluxe line.

For a slightly different look when considering #4/worsted-weight yarns, consider Deluxe Worsted Tweed. It offers the same twist and gauge as the Deluxe Worsted and Deluxe Worsted Superwash.

Fibra Natura Donnina, also from Universal Yarn, is the lighter-weight cousin to Dona. When held double it works up nicely as a #4/worsted-weight yarn; alone, it excels as a #1/fingering-weight yarn. When a substitute is needed in superwash extra-fine merino, it's a flexible yarn to work into your yarn plan. I prefer it to #4/worsted-weight yarn when I want a warmer layer next to the skin because holding it double provides a nice lofty pocket in which air can be trapped to keep the person wearing my fiber creation just a little bit warmer when the winter winds howl.

If Universal Yarn Deluxe Worsted is not available, Patons Classic Wool will work for the #4/worsted-weight patterns in this collection. It is a reliable three-ply #4/worsted-weight 100% wool yarn with properties similar to the Universal Yarn Deluxe Worsted. Color selection varies by retail outlet and website.

For a #4/worsted-weight vegan option, Universal Yarn Cotton Supreme is available in an impressive range of colors and—like its #3/DK-weight cousin—it too will hold a cable nicely, so it's a welcome addition for textured knitting. As one would expect with cotton, it is a bit more dense than the #4/worsted-weight wool and acrylic options already discussed.

Deluxe Bulky Superwash
Used for: San Francisco Cabled Cowl (page 49)
Deluxe Bulky Superwash is available in 106 yd/97 m per 3.5 oz/100 g skeins, which make it just the right amount of yarn for a knit hat, cowl, or pair of mittens. Substitutions for it must be carefully considered. The closest substitute I have found is Cozy Color Works Bulky. For the cowl featured in this collection and any other piece of fiber art requiring frequent washing, superwash wool is preferable to non-superwash. When substituting other yarns for Universal Yarn Deluxe Bulky Superwash, consider the number of plies, texture, and construction of the yarn.

Yarn Bee Authentic Hand-Dyed Chunky is a lovely alternative with similar characteristics and yardage, 110 yd/106 m per 3.5 oz/100 g skein. Universal Yarn Uptown Super Bulky is a perfect alternative for those projects where wool is not desirable. Uptown comes in a wide range of colors, and while the Uptown Super Bulky is a bit more dense than Deluxe Bulky Superwash, it can be worked at a similar gauge and it too will hold a stitch pattern well.

With all this in mind, embrace experimentation. Good luck and happy swatching!

Swatching

Swatching is like reading the directions all the way through before tackling a project. It just makes sense to do it so there are no big surprises after an investment of resources and time.

We swatch to find a common measurement on which to base our projects. No two knitters will knit at exactly the same gauge every time they settle in to work on a new project; therefore designers provide a suggested gauge at which to work. Without gauge, the number of stitches to cast on, number of rows to knit, and finished dimensions are irrelevant unless one relies strictly on linear measurements. Making a swatch frames the parameters of your finished project by allowing you as the creator to give the project your own individual knitting style while affording you some level of security that you will produce results aligned with the outcome the designer intended if you work at the same gauge with similar materials, and follow the pattern directions.

The combination of row count and stitch count can be difficult to achieve. For patterns in this collection, if you find your row gauge with one needle size and stitch gauge at a different needle size, I recommend you use the needle that yielded the desired stitch gauge because the row gauge for projects in this collection are less relevant than the stitch gauge. If you find you are closely aligned but cannot get the correct gauge, try using a different pair of needles.

Some combinations of needles and yarn are more compatible than others. For example, if you find your gauge is a bit too loose with a pair of metal needles, a wooden set at the same size may provide just enough friction to hold the yarn and create a tighter fabric. Since most of the work to create a knit or purl stitch takes place toward the tip of the needles, changing to a different tip can also be useful when attempting to work at the desired gauge.

Pro Tip: Read the entire pattern before picking up your needles. There could be critical information hidden in a caption, footnote, or pattern note that may be useful to get the correct gauge.

If after multiple attempts to create a swatch at the desired gauge you are still unable to "get gauge," try tensioning the yarn through different fingers to see if it improves your ability to match the designer's gauge.

CREATING A GAUGE SWATCH

Begin by using the needles as suggested in the pattern and knit a swatch in the yarn you envision using for the project using the combination of needle size and stitch in which the gauge is stated in the pattern. If the pattern is worked in the round and the gauge does not state otherwise, the gauge as stated is in the round, so make sure you knit your gauge swatch in the round.

Pro Tip: Most patterns state gauge in terms of the number of stitches and rows required to create a 4-inch/10-centimeter square. Because knit stitches tend to roll on themselves, it can be very difficult to accurately measure the gauge of a swatch. Rather than fight it, double the number of stitches in the swatch with the goal of creating an 8-inch/20-centimeter square.

Once the swatch is completed, place your measuring device in the middle of the swatch. While it may be tempting to just drop a tape measure across the work, this may result in a less accurate measurement as the fabric and tape glide across each other. It is better to use a rigid tool or ruler. I prefer to use a tool that allows me to measure both row and stitch count at the same time. As with a tape measure, the process of measuring stitch count with a ruler and then repositioning the ruler to measure the row gauge can produce inaccurate results. Measuring both at once provides more accurate row and stitch counts. If the gauge is close or close enough, it is time to wash the swatch to check its resilience over time. If the gauge is off, step up or down needle sizes until more favorable results are created.

If there are too many stitches over the stated field, likely a 4-inch/10-centimeter square, make another swatch using a larger pair of needles. If there are too few stitches, make another swatch using a smaller pair of needles.

Pro Tip: When determining which swatch is most closely aligned with your envisioned results, it is best to have all your swatches close at hand to compare and contrast. If you have enough yarn or multiple skeins available, don't reuse the same yarn for every swatch, and do not cut the working yarn between swatches. Once you settle on a particular gauge, simply undo the stitches from the other swatches and return the yarn to the cake or ball from which it was knit.

After achieving the desired gauge in the unblocked swatch, wash it per the ball band instructions and when it is dry, measure it again. If it retains its shape and provides you with the blocked or desired gauge, you are ready to start your project. If it does not, try blocking it to see if it can be manipulated to the correct gauge, or make another swatch using a different pair of needles in a different size.

If your pattern states the gauge when blocked, it is likely because the final gauge of the finished piece is significantly different than the gauge suggested on the yarn label. For example, a pattern may specify the gauge of a sock-weight yarn on US size 8/5 mm needles to knit up at a gauge of 18 stitches and 24 rows to create a 4-inch/10-centimeter square, even though the label on that same yarn states a suggested needle size of US size 2/2.75 mm to produce a swatch of the same size at a gauge of approximately 30 stitches and 32 rows.

Pro Tip: If you observe that the gauge in the pattern and on the ball band are significantly different, check the pattern notes to ascertain at what point in the swatching process the gauge is measured. When in doubt, ask for advice from the local yarn store where the yarn was purchased.

The bigger the difference between your swatch and that of the pattern, the bigger the difference between your finished item and the one in the pattern will be.

TROUBLESHOOTING

Gauge is off by less than 2 sts per inch: A knitting needle will produce results based upon how it is used, what it is made out of, how much it weighs, and the general shape of the tip. Changing one of these factors by switching needles may help you get the desired gauge using the same size needle. So, if your gauge is very close to the stated gauge of the pattern—within a stitch/row or two—try a different pair of needles the same size from a different collection to see if a slight difference in tip, weight, or needle material produces the desired results.

Pro Tip: Knitting needle sizes across brands are not always consistent. For instance, a US 2 from one manufacturer might be 2.5 mm and from another 2.75 mm. Patterns typically list both US size and metric size, so check to be sure that your intended needles match both sizes.

Too many stitches: Make another swatch using a larger size needle. The needles you are using are too small and require the yarn to be worked too many times to produce the number of stitches required per inch.

Too few stitches: Make another swatch using a smaller size needle. The ones you are using are producing a fabric that is too open or loose.

Swatch just feels wrong: If you substitute another yarn for the yarn specified in the pattern, your gauge or the hand of the fabric may not match that of the pattern. When substituting one fiber for another, it is important to understand how the two differ before attempting to reconcile the gauge produced versus the gauge stated in the pattern. Even when the same gauge is achieved using a different yarn, the finished product may yield different results than that of the original.

Pro Tip: When substituting yarns, make sure the yarn you are considering is as close as possible in weight, meterage, composition, and hand as the original. A #3/DK-weight cotton chainette will not produce the same results as a #3/DK-weight four-ply wool blend.

MAKING A GAUGE SWATCH IN THE ROUND

Working a gauge swatch in the round is critical if your pattern gauge is stated in the round. For most people, there is some slight difference in the way the yarn is tensioned on right-side versus wrong-side rows. Because the same side is always facing when working in the round, it is critical to check your gauge in the round for a perfect fit. Swatching in the round is similar to making an I-cord: the right side of the work is always facing you, and the yarn is carried behind the work on the wrong side when the work is shifted to the opposite side of the double-pointed needle or circular needle.

1. Read the entire pattern, making sure the gauge as stated is in fact measured in the round.
2. Gather your supplies:
   - Gauge tool
   - Two stitch markers
   - Appropriate circular needle or double-pointed needles
   - Project yarn

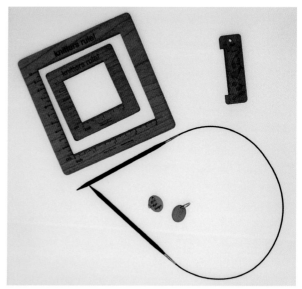

Always swatch with the type of needle you will use for the project and check your gauge carefully using a gauge tool. Shown here are my go-to gauge tools from Katrinkles, markers, and a circular needle.

3. Using the needles and yarn you would like to use for the majority of the project and for which the gauge is stated in the appropriate style, cast on five stitches, place a marker, cast on double the number of stitches stated for the gauge swatch, place a marker, knit five extra stitches.

4. Knit across, slipping markers as you come to them.

5. Slide the stitches to the other end of the needle.

A long-tail cast-on was used; therefore, at the end of the first row, the tail is at the opposite end of the needle, away from the working yarn. Notice the tail of the yarn, gathered together into a small bow to highlight its location, is back near the stitch that will be worked first for the next row/round. It will be on this side of the work, as every row is knit because the work is never turned; it is slid from one side of the needle to the other so all work is done with the right side facing.

6. Carry the working yarn behind/under the work back to the position to work the first stitch.

7. With the right side facing, knit the first five stitches, slip the marker, work two sets in gauge pattern stitch, slip the marker, knit five stitches.

Here I have begun to knit the second row/round, having just slipped the marker and started the pattern stitches.

Having just completed the second row/round of the swatch, the working yarn is shown near the tip of the needle and the tail is at the opposite end of the work. The piece of yarn in the middle just below the row worked is the slack that was left in the yarn when it was slid into position to work the row.

8. Repeat steps 4 to 7 until the swatch is complete, about twice as long as the length of the suggested gauge swatch in the pattern. There will be loops of unworked slack yarn across the back. The measurement of the gauge will not include the slack yarn or the stitches, which are denoted as the first and last five on the swatch.

Completing the last row/round of swatch. Notice that the tail is consistently present in the same corner, at the lower right in this example, as all swatching is done on the right side of the work.

9. Remove the work from the needle.
10. Lay the work flat with the right side facing up and the unworked loops underneath it.
11. Measure the gauge between the stitch markers at a couple of different points in the swatch. Measure the gauge toward the middle of the work, not at the edges.
12. If the gauge is close to the desired outcome, wash the swatch and block it. After it is dry, cut the tails off the back and check the gauge a second time. If the blocked gauge is not correct, block it again or make another one on a larger or smaller set of needles.

If the gauge swatch is not close to the desired results, make another swatch on a larger or smaller set of needles and measure again.

Blocking

Blocking, like swatching, seems to be unpopular with many fiber artists, and I don't understand why. The process of blocking a finished piece sets the size and evens out the stitch work. It can transform a piece entirely from homemade craft to handmade art. Blocking allows the yarn you just lovingly worked through your own fingers over the needles into a beautiful, finished piece to relax and realize its full potential. Whether to simply tidy up a bit of uneven tension, make a panel a particular size, or open up delicate lace work, blocking is a critical last step in your knitting journey.

Before blocking your finished piece, think about the reasoning behind blocking it and use the right equipment for the job. Blocking boards, pins, wires, T-pins, and a wide range of other notions are available to make the job easier (or more complicated, depending upon your point of view).

At a basic level, blocking helps relax the fibers and create a more cohesive fabric. Blocking a panel with straight sides evens out the edges. This is helpful when pieces need to be seamed together as it gives you a more even edge along which to sew the seam. When blocking a piece that does not require seaming, the process of blocking it allows the fabric to be manipulated into its final shape.

Contrary to popular belief, blocking does not require a large number of task-specific tools. The blocking for all the pieces in this collection was done using bath towels, a fan, candy thermometer, tape measure, clothes steamer, yoga mat, and either blocking wires with pins or knit blockers. I prefer using yoga mats rather than blocking mats or other modular plastic mats because there are fewer seams in the surface on which I am working, and keeping a yoga mat clean is a lot easier than keeping every corner and tongue in a set of blocking mats free of debris that might otherwise stick to my knitted creation.

The best way to test the blocking method you would like to use for a given item is to block the swatch. Swatch blocking gives you the opportunity to learn how a given stitch and yarn combination will respond to initial blocking and future care.

Pro Tip: Yarn companies may not always source their materials consistently for the entire life of a product. When sources change, the behavior of the finished product is also subject to change. So even a yarn with which you worked previously may not respond the way it has in the past. In short, always swatch your yarn and block the swatch to get a more complete understanding of how a given yarn and stitch will pair.

To aid in the process of blocking the pieces in this collection, the First Byte Design crew of test knitters added suggested notions and blocking techniques in the Finishing section of patterns where we thought you might find them helpful. Your blocking method and notions needed will be based upon the yarn used, available space, and your personal preferences.

BLOCKING YARNS THAT CAN BE MACHINE WASHED OR HAND WASHED

To begin, fill a basin or bucket with water no warmer than the temperature the yarn band indicates is suitable for the yarn. If you are a real stickler for detail, like me, use the candy thermometer to make sure you are using the water at the right temperature. Place your finished piece in the water. To lessen the chance of felting, allow it to sink into the basin rather than pushing it under the water. The less manipulation, the better. If after 20 minutes the piece does not sink, gently assist it to sink to the bottom of the basin and allow it to rest there for 20 minutes.

An item made of superwash yarn should then be put into the clothes dryer on low heat to remove some of the moisture prior to blocking. Any other piece that is more than slightly damp should be placed on a towel, flat with no creases, with a second towel over it. Roll the towels together with the piece in between. Working from one end of the rolled-up towel, gently press the roll in your hands to squeeze the water out. This will prevent the piece from accidentally felting as the water is removed from it. Do not wring it out, as this may cause unnecessary strain on the fabric. Unroll the towels and continue with just your finished piece. If the piece still seems too wet, repeat this step with another set of towels.

Unfurl the yoga mat and remove any incidental dust or other contaminants from it. If the mat tends to roll up, place small heavy items on the corners to keep the surface flat.

Pro Tip: Blocking should be done on a floor or counter. If neither is suitable, a mattress will work; however it is best to put down a sheet of plywood over the mattress first to maintain a level surface on which to work.

Place the slightly damp piece on the yoga mat and begin to flatten it out, stretching it slightly to the desired finished dimensions. Proceed based on whether you are using pins and blocking wires or knit blockers.

Option A: Pins and Blocking Wires

Insert the blocking wires into the edges of the finished piece and gently manipulate the wires through the entire length of the first selvedge edge, second selvedge edge, cast-on row, and bind-off row, one wire or more per side. While a blocking wire can be used to create a curve, do not attempt to bend a blocking wire to create sharp corners—it will not be easy to manipulate and will not produce the desired result of neatening the edge of the fabric. If a blocking wire is not long enough, multiple wires can be used on a side, or a longer wire can be used. Blocking wires are typically stainless steel and approximately 30 inches long, so if a longer length is desired, overlap them by approximately 3 inches and secure them to the blocking board at both ends (and twice at any point where they are overlapped) to keep them aligned. If an alternative wire is used, be sure that it will not rust and leave stains on your project.

Using blocking T-pins, secure the piece to the yoga mat by passing the T-pins through the blocking wires between the blocking wire and the finished piece. Proper T-pin placement prevents the T-pins from tearing the edges or creating undesirable undulations along the finished edge. Blockers may be used in lieu of T-pins if preferred. For households with pets and children, I strongly recommend using blockers instead of T-pins because blockers are larger and less likely to be swallowed by a pet or an unsupervised child.

Option B: Knit Blockers

Lay the piece out on the mat, adjusting the fabric with your fingers to manipulate it into the final dimensions. Using the smallest blockers, secure the corners of your work to the mat. Using the larger blockers, secure the sides of your work. The precise number of blockers used is based upon the size, weight, shape, and amount of manipulation necessary to hold the work in place while it dries.

Measure the sides of the work after manipulating the stitches. If necessary, repeat the blocking process to manipulate the fabric again.

When measuring the final piece, if it has square corners, I always double-check my corners using an architect's triangle or quilter's square.

Lightly steam the piece before it is dry. Use a blunt needle or knitting needle to adjust any abnormally tight or loose stitches.

Allow the piece to air dry. If the process of drying the fabric needs to be shortened, a fan is preferable to direct sunlight or heat. Any portable fan will do the job. It is best to not use heat as heat may cause the knitted fabric to respond unfavorably. The fan I use is a squirrel fan, available from any home improvement store.

After the piece has dried, remove it from the mat and put away the blockers or pins and wires.

Pro Tip: Before you start, write down how many blockers, pins, and wires were used and verify that you have all of them off the mat before you put it away.

Check that the mat itself is dry before putting it away. Hanging it over a door or shower rod will allow air to circulate more freely through it and facilitate the drying process.

Review the piece and work in any loose ends that may have developed as a result of the blocking process. Use a tapestry needle to weave in ends that may require detailed manipulation.

YARN THAT CANNOT BE MACHINE OR HAND WASHED

In most cases, yarn can be steam blocked even if it is not machine or hand washable. Before applying any moisture to a finished piece made from non-washable yarn, try blocking a swatch approximately 8 inches (20 centimeters) square in the pattern stitch to verify whether the yarn can be steamed. After testing the swatch, in lieu of setting the finished piece into a basin of water, lay it out on a yoga mat and use steam from a clothes steamer to relax the stitches. An iron on the steam setting may be used instead of a steamer; however, the iron should not touch the fabric as it may compress, burn, or melt it. If an iron is used, it is best to place a piece of lightweight cotton muslin between it and the finished piece to reduce the possibility of melting or burning the yarn.

Once the fabric is relaxed and still warm to the touch, begin pinning it to the mat into the desired shape and dimensions.

Measure the sides of the work after manipulating the stitches. If necessary, repeat the blocking process to manipulate the fabric again.

When measuring the final piece, if it has square corners, I always double-check my corners using an architect's triangle or quilter's square.

Lightly steam the piece before it is dry. Use a blunt needle or knitting needle to adjust any abnormally tight or loose stitches.

Allow the piece to air dry. If the process of drying the fabric needs to be shortened, a fan is preferable to direct sunlight or heat. Any portable fan will do the job. It is best to not use heat as heat may cause the knitted fabric to respond unfavorably. The fan I use is a squirrel fan, available from any home improvement store.

After the piece has dried, remove it from the mat and put away the blockers or pins and wires.

Pro Tip: Before you start, write down how many blockers, pins, and wires were used and verify that you have all of them off the mat before you put it away.

Check that the mat itself is dry before putting it away. Hanging it over a door or shower rod will allow air to circulate more freely through it and facilitate the drying process.

Review the piece and work in any loose ends that may have developed as a result of the blocking process. Use a tapestry needle to weave ends that may require detailed manipulation.

TROUBLESHOOTING

Garment will not block or maintain desired shape: Yarns that lack memory will not respond well to blocking. Wool, superwash wool, and other animal fibers like alpaca and cashmere have some ability to retain their final shape after blocking because the fibers themselves have a slight halo of fibers surrounding the yarn itself. Bamboo, cotton, viscose, rayon, linen, and silk lack the ability to retain their shape well because they tend to be smoother yarns and do not have the halo of fibers to help the fabric keep its shape.

Pro Tip: If you have trouble blocking a given yarn, ask the manufacturer for guidance.

Color run: Some yarns are more prone to running than others. There are ways to mitigate color release from your yarn; all are best explored on swatches rather than your finished garment.

One cup of vinegar or citric acid mixed in with the soaking water should set any dye remaining in your fabric. To stop the color from running out of the fabric, it may have to rest in the soak and be rinsed several times. Once the rinse water no longer contains dye, you know that the remaining dye is set.

Pro Tip: Use the warmest water the yarn can tolerate, and each time the item is soaked, use a fresh batch of vinegar and water of the same temperature as the rinse water to prevent felting or other undesirable results.

Resist the temptation to expedite the process by using hot water. Hot water may cause the yarn to shrink and cause excessive color bleed. Between soakings, remove as much water as possible by laying the piece in between two towels and gently squeezing it to remove the water without damaging the fabric itself.

Pro Tip: Use old towels when rolling your swatch or finished piece to remove excess water, as un-set dye may permanently stain.

Citric acid used in combination with heat can set dye. This is not my favorite method because yarn can combust or melt under the right circumstances. Proceed with extreme caution if you elect to try using a citric acid bath in the microwave, and do not use the family microwave for this as some dyes are not food safe.

Commercially available items like Shout Color Catchers will deter color run on machine-washable items. If laying the items in a vinegar bath does not remove all the excess dye, fabric knit using washable yarns can be put into the washing machine on a delicate setting with the appropriate water temperature and a color catcher.

Finished piece not big enough or too big after blocking: The larger the discrepancy between your final dimensions and the pattern dimensions, the higher the likelihood the yarn did not behave as expected. This can be due to fluctuations in gauge, a change in yarn, or fiber shrinkage during the blocking process.

Blocking is a part of the knitting process; it is not a fix-all. If a piece is too small after blocking, check the gauge of the piece versus that of the pattern to see if perhaps you did not block it aggressively enough to open up the stitches as the designer intended. If this is the case, try blocking it again.

If the finished item is too large, it could be due to the way in which it was prepared prior to blocking. The gauge could be incorrect, or the pairing of yarn and pattern stitch may not be ideal.

Pro Tip: Superwash wool does not have the ability to "spring back" into its original shape. When wet it tends to become shapeless, and stretches in a surprising number of directions. To remediate this, it needs to be dried or at least partially dried before troubleshooting can begin in earnest.

Regardless of the material used for your projects, to avoid unintended issues with sizing, always make at least one gauge swatch, measure the gauge, block it, and measure it again. For a little extra insurance, check the math in the pattern itself as you work. For instance, if the gauge is 5 stitches to the inch and calls for a 40-stitch cast-on, that edge should be 8 inches. If it is not, it could be because there was a mistake in the pattern, or the yarn is not performing as expected. Before proceeding to "see what happens," stop, try to cast on again, and if the issue persists, contact the publisher of the pattern for guidance. Patterns go through an iterative process from conception to publication, during which time errors can make their way into even the best work.

Pro Tip: Designers do not test knit every single size of every single pattern. In most cases one or two tests are done at different sizes, and the others are derived mathematically from test knits. So, while care is taken to validate every pattern, no one is perfect, and occasionally an error is found after a pattern is published.

A Note on Bias Twist

Plied yarn is a compilation of fibers spun together to create a thicker yarn than any one of the plies itself. If a yarn is spun too tightly, it can create a fabric that is twisted, an effect known as "bias." This error in manufacture causes an otherwise square piece of fabric to present as a trapezoid or other non-square shape. The larger your swatch, the easier it is to predict whether a bias twist will present itself in your finished garment. Yarn that bears this manufacturing defect should be used for other purposes; it will never produce a reliable finished garment. It may be suitable for an accessory like a scarf. Do not waste your time attempting to untwist poorly manufactured yarn. It is better suited for use as gift wrap ribbon or making pom-poms. It can also be cut into small pieces to make stuffing.

Technique Guide

I use a few standard techniques that are easy to do but can be tricky to remember without a refresher. Following are step-by-step tutorials for the provisional cast-on, Kitchener stitch, and three-needle bind-off.

PROVISIONAL CAST-ON

A provisional cast-on is very useful when the visual presence of a seam is not desired or when working a piece in two different directions. It is created by working a row of stitches in the project yarn into a crochet chain worked in waste yarn, and later removing the chain to join the live stitches to another set of live stitches or to then work in the opposite direction. The basics are as follows:

1. Using a crochet hook of similar diameter to the knitting needles, create a crochet chain using a piece of scrap yarn approximately 10 stitches longer than the desired number of stitches you wish to cast on. These extra 10 chain stitches are helpful in case you miss one when casting on the knit stitches and to hold onto as you work the stitches toward the end of the row.
2. Place a locking stitch marker through the last chain stitch to prevent it from working itself loose. It can be knotted or fastened off if a stitch marker is not available.
3. Rotate the chain in your left hand such that you can see the bumps on the back of it, not the "v" that looks like a knit stitch—that part you want to leave. Stitches are going to be worked into the back bump (behind the "v"). Using a knitting needle and the working yarn, pull a stitch through the loop formed between the bump in the back of the chain and the "v" on the front. Each loop made using the working yarn will count as a stitch.

4. Repeat step 3 until the desired number of loops are present on the knitting needle. They will not look like a knit or a purl stitch at this point. Begin working on the pattern as presented and ignore the chain until the directions tell you to remove it.
5. Remove the chain by opening the locking stitch marker and slowly unraveling the chain. As the chains are removed, the knitted stitches are live stitches, which must be captured on a stitch holder or spare needle.
6. Continue working pattern as directed.

KITCHENER STITCH

For times when you want a seam that is barely visible to the experienced knitter, and invisible to most other people, Kitchener is the stitch to use. When you get the tension just right, it's very hard to see it in a sea of stockinette. It works when there are two pieces of knit fabric with the same number of stitches on them.

Pro Tip: If you need to join two pieces invisibly, and there are more stitches on one piece than the other, bind off in pattern until you have the same number of stitches on each piece or work the last few rows of each piece using hidden decreases until you get to the right number of stitches on each piece.

There are only four steps to the Kitchener stitch. Once you get the two setup steps done, it's a lot easier to just think about the four steps you will repeat on the live stitches to join them.

Holding the two pieces with the RS facing out on the needles, WS together on the inside, align the two needles together in your left hand parallel to each other with the tips holding the stitches facing to the right.

Using a tapestry needle and piece of yarn from the working yarn approximately four times longer than the seam I want to make, I insert the needle through the first stitch on the front needle purlwise and draw the yarn through. After each step, I draw the yarn through, so I won't bore you by telling you to do that every time. Insert the needle through the first stitch in the back knitwise, and leave it on the needle.

Now we're all settled in to just do the next four steps until all the stitches are bound off. There are a few tips to make it easier, which I tend to mumble to myself when I do Kitchener stitch.

On odd steps, you slip the stitch off the needle; on even steps you leave it on.

Too much to remember? Our knitting buddies at Katrinkles made a perfect little tool so you don't have to (see page 6)!

1. Push the tapestry needle through the first stitch on the front knitting needle knitwise, and slip the stitch off the knitting needle. That stitch is done, not worked again.
2. Push the tapestry needle through the stitch on the front knitting needle as if to purl, and leave it on the knitting needle. You need it for step 1 the next time through.
3. Push the tapestry needle through the stitch on the back knitting needle purlwise, and slip the stitch off the needle. That stitch is done, not worked again.
4. Push the tapestry needle through stitch on back knitting needle knitwise, and leave it on the knitting needle. It will get slipped off the next time through.

THREE-NEEDLE BIND-OFF

A three-needle bind-off builds a seam that can be a decorative and structural element when worked on the right side of a piece of knitwear or a structural element on the wrong side of the fabric. The stitches to be seamed should be on separate needles or on the opposite ends of a circular needle. You will need one extra needle to manipulate the stitches; typically this needle is the same size as the needles on which the stitches are positioned.

Holding the two pieces with the same side facing out—both RS or both WS as directed in the pattern—align the two needles so they are parallel to each other in your left hand with the tips facing to the right. Most of the time you will be creating this seam on the WS of the fabric, so the WS of both fabrics will be facing out and the RS are touching each other. The steps are the same either way.

1. Using the working yarn, holding the third needle in your right hand, insert the tip of the right needle through the first stitch on the front needle in your left hand and continue to push the third needle through the corresponding stitch on the back needle in your left hand as if you are going to knit them both together—which is exactly what you will do next. Using the working yarn, wrap the yarn around the tip of the third needle and knit these two stitches together, allowing them to slip off the left needles on which they were previously positioned. One stitch is now on the right needle and one less stitch is on each of the needles in your left hand.
2. Repeat step 1; there are now two stitches on the right needle.
3. Using either of the two needles in your left hand, manipulate the stitch on the right needle you made in step 1 over the stitch you made in step 2 as if you were binding the first stitch off and allow it to drop off the needle, keeping the stitch from step 2 on the needle.
4. Repeat steps 2 and 3 until all the stitches are removed from the left needles and one remains on the right needle.
5. Pull the working yarn through the last stitch on the right needle and weave in the end.

Abbreviations

C1F	cable 1 stitch front; slip 1 stitch to working needle, knit next stitch, pass slipped stitch back to left needle in front of stitch, and knit this stitch
C2F	cable 2 stitches with stitches held in front of the work; place 2 stitches on the cable needle, knit 2, return stitches to left needle, knit these 2 stitches
C3F	cable 3 stitches with stitches held in front of the work; place 3 stitches on the cable needle, knit 3, return stitches to the left needle, knit these 3 stitches
CC	contrasting color
dec	decrease(d)
DPNs	double-pointed needles
inc	increase(d)
k	knit
k2tog	knit 2 stitches together (decrease one stitch)
k2togtbl	knit two stitches together through the back of the loop (decrease one stitch)
kfb	knit into the front of the stitch and the back of the same stitch (increase one stitch)
m	marker
MC	main color
M1	make one stitch
M1L	make one left-leaning stitch; insert the left needle from front to back under the strand connecting the last stitch on the left needle and the stitch just worked on the right needle. Knit this segment of yarn through the back of the loop.

M1p	make one purl stitch; on the wrong side of the fabric, insert the left needle under the strand between the last stitch on the left needle and the stitch just worked from back to front. Insert the right needle into the front of the loop just placed on the left-hand needle and purl the strand.
M1R	make one right-leaning stitch; insert the left needle under the strand between the last stitch on the left needle and the stitch just worked from back to front. Insert the right needle into this strand from front to back (knitwise) and knit.
P	purl
pbf	purl into the back and front of the same stitch (increase one stitch)
PC2B	holding the yarn on the WS of the work, slip next 2 stitches to cable needle and hold these 2 stitches on RS of the work, p2, p2 from cable needle.
pm	place marker
RS	right side
sl	slip
sl1wyif	slip 1 stitch with yarn in front
sl3wyif	slip 3 stitches with yarn in front
sm	slip marker
st	stitch
sts	stitches
tbl	through the back of the loop
WS	wrong side
wyib	with yarn in back
wyif	with yarn in front
yo	yarn over

Patterns

Delaware River Mitts

Between New Jersey and Pennsylvania, the Delaware River hugs the border on its journey to Wilmington, Delaware, and into the Atlantic Ocean. Two towpaths, long since abandoned for transport, can be used for hours of leisurely cycling along the banks of the river. In the spring, the river is alive with a bit of ice and the bounty of melting snow; it is the perfect time to visit, albeit a bit chilly in the mornings. Whether you decide to begin your journey where the Delaware starts up north in New York or closer to Point Breeze, New Jersey, the ride is well worth it. My favorite spot to start is in New Hope, Pennsylvania, not far from where George Washington crossed the Delaware one fateful Christmas Eve.

These mitts are a quick project designed to allow you, the maker and creator, to personalize them to suit the hands they will envelop in a smooth silken layer of warmth. They are perfect for turning gears as you cycle along the towpath or settle in to turn a few pages of your favorite book. The yarn itself, Universal Yarn Wool Pop, is a sturdy blend of bamboo, wool, and polyamide spun into a soft, springy yarn, perfect for accessories and blankets. Wool Pop is available in a wide range of colors. Waterfall, used here, has a white ply running through it because one of the fibers did not take the dye in the same way as the others. Other colors of Wool Pop, like red, are tonal in a very subtle way. Whichever color you choose, Wool Pop will not disappoint. It is easy to care for and comfortable for year-round knitwear.

Mitts, like cowls, make good gifts because they are easy to mail and need not have the precise fit of a sweater. Keep a pair in your tote to work a few rounds here and there throughout your day, and before long, you will have a pair.

Pro Tip: When knitting on the road, make the two thumbs first, put them on stitch holders, and then start the body of the mitts. You'll have less fiddling on the go with pieces and part construction if you do the basics at home and just work the rounds on the road.

Knit from the top down, the mitts can easily be modified to suit the available yardage. The pair as shown uses 1.3 oz/38 g of Universal Yarn Wool Pop, so from a single hank you can get two pairs—making it a wise choice for budget-friendly knitting enjoyment.

As you catch up with girlfriends on the balcony while the boys play touch football, this pair of mitts will keep your look picture-perfect.

Yarn

Universal Yarn Wool Pop (50% bamboo, 35% superwash wool, 15% polyamide); 284 yd/260 m per 3.5 oz/100 g skein; Color: 629 Waterfall, 1 skein

Dimensions

7"/18 cm cast-on to cuff, 7"/18 cm circumference (stretches to suit up to woman's size 9 hand), blocked

Gauge

30 sts × 25 rows = 4"/10 cm square in pattern stitch, worked in the round, unblocked, using the larger needle

Needles

US size 5/3.75 mm 9"/23 cm circular, US size 7/4.5 mm 9"/23 cm circular

Notions

2 stitch markers (one for beginning of round, the other for the Thumb gusset), darning needle, stitch counter

Pattern Notes

- These mitts are constructed using a top-down method. Since the pattern is worked from the top down, the length can be easily adjusted for a smaller hand or shorter forearm length by varying the number of rounds completed.
- To optimize the utility of your skein, you may elect to weigh the skein and divide it into two balls of yarn rather than work the first, then the second mitt from one ball.
- Consider the pattern repeat if you elect to change the length of your mitts. Each cable twist in pattern at gauge using the US size 7/4.5 mm needle is ¾"/2 cm when measured from the top of the cable twist of one to the bottom of the next. When making a longer pair of mitts, I recommend that you add the length after attaching the thumb to reduce the likelihood of a misalignment between the thumb and body of the mitt.
- If 9"/23 cm circular needles are not available, DPNs may be substituted. While the work can be done using the magic loop, the test knitters found it difficult to attach the Thumb when using the magic loop technique.

INSTRUCTIONS

Thumb, knit flat (Make 2)

Using US size 5/3.75 mm needle, cast on 16 stitches.

Row 1 (RS): P1 *k2, p1, repeat from * to end of row.
Row 2 (WS): K1 *p2, k1, repeat from * to end of row.

Soft and velvety against the skin, Wool Pop is an ideal yarn for accessories.

Change to US size 7/4.5 mm needle and continue as follows:

Row 3: P1 *k2, p1, repeat from * to end of row.
Row 4: P1 *C1F, p1, repeat from * to end of row.
Row 5: K1 *p2, k1, repeat from * to end of row.

Set Thumb aside on stitch holder or extra needle and work on the Body.

Body, knit in the round (Make 2)

Using the US size 5/3.75 mm needle, cast on 45 stitches.

Place marker and join in the round.

Rounds 1 and 2 (RS): *K2, p1, repeat from * to end of round.
Rounds 3 and 4: Change to US size 7/4.5 mm needle, repeat round 1.
Round 5: *C1F, p1, repeat from * to end of round.
Rounds 6–8: *K2, p1, repeat from * to end of round.

Round 9: *C1F, p1, repeat from * to end of round.
Round 10: Repeat round 5 omitting the final p1, leaving it on the left needle. (44 sts worked)
Round 11: Add the Thumb stitches to the left needle, p1, place marker; work next 14 of the Thumb stitches as they present themselves, working them to the right needle with the working yarn from the Body. Slip 16th stitch of the Thumb to right needle, remove the marker on the left needle, slip stitch back to left needle, purl this 16th stitch (last Thumb stitch) together with the purl stitch from the last round of the Body, replace the marker between the p2tog and the first knit stitch on the left needle. The beginning of round/first marker from the Body of the mitt will now be between the p2tog and the knit stitch on the left needle. Going forward, the new marker is the beginning of round marker and the first marker originally placed on the Body, as its end of round marker will be the Thumb marker. (1 st dec)

Knit from the top down, the Delaware River Mitts can be tailored for the perfect fit.

Round 12: *K2, p1, repeat from * to end of round, slipping Thumb marker as you come to it.

Round 13: *C1F, p1, repeat from * to end of round, slipping markers as you come to them.

Rounds 14–16: Repeat round 12.

Round 17: *C1F, p1, repeat from * to end of round, slipping markers as you come to them.

Round 18: Sm, ssk, *p1, k2, repeat from * three times, p1, k2tog, p1, sm **k2, p1, repeat from ** to end of round. (2 sts dec)

Rounds 19, 23, and 27: Continue in pattern with no decreases.

Round 20: Sm, ssk, *k2, p1* twice, k2, k2tog, p1, sm, **k2, p1, repeat from ** to end of round. (2 sts dec)

Round 21: Sm, k1, C1F, p1, C1F, p1, C1F, k1, p1, sm, *C1F, p1, repeat from * to end of round.

Round 22: Sm, ssk, k1, p1, k2, p1, k1, k2tog, p1, sm, *k2, p1, repeat from * to end of round. (2 sts dec)

Round 24: Sm, ssk, p1, k2, p1, k2tog, p1, sm *k2, p1, repeat from * to end of round. (2 sts dec)

Round 25: Sm, k1, p1, C1F, p1, k1, p1, sm *C1F, p1, repeat from * to end of round.

Round 26: Sm, ssk, k2, p1, k2tog, sm *k2, p1, repeat from * to end of round. (2 sts dec)

Round 28: Sm, ssk, k1, k2tog, sm *k2, p1, repeat from * to end of round. (2 sts dec)

Round 29: Sm, k3, sm, *C1F, p1, repeat from * to end of round.

Round 30: Sm, k3tog, sm, *k2, p1, repeat from * to end of round, remove marker, slip the k3tog from the beginning of the round over the purl. (45 sts remain)

Rounds 31–32: *K2, p1, repeat from * to end of round.

Round 33: *C1F, p1, repeat from * to end of round.
Rounds 34–36: *K2, p1, repeat from * to end of round.

Repeat rounds 33–36 until you have reached the end of the yarn or desired length. Bind off in pattern after a round 36. To keep the edge from flaring out due to the cable splay, switch to the smaller needle for the final round 34–36 repeats.

Finishing

Sew seam along the inside of the Thumb using the tail of the long-tail cast-on.

Weave in ends.

Wash per ball band directions.

Revisit ends to make sure none revealed themselves during washing and blocking.

Enjoy your new mitts.

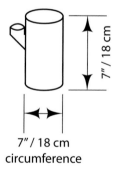

7" / 18 cm circumference

7" / 18 cm cast-on to cuff, 7" / 18 cm circumference, stretches to suit up to woman's size 9 hand

Oyster Creek Mitts

These mitts with their gently undulating textured stitch were inspired by a gently flowing river that meanders from Chatham, Massachusetts, to Nantucket Sound. The water is not very deep, the perfect haven for migrating wildlife or a canoe trip. In the late spring as the flowers begin to bloom, before the crowds flock to the coast, a warm hat and pair of mitts will be much appreciated on late afternoon walks. For added durability when foraging for shells or picking wildflowers, these mitts were designed with ease of care in mind, using Universal Yarn Worsted Superwash.

If your travels bring you here, these mitts will bring you back. For a complementary project, check out the Nantucket Tradewinds Hat (page 67) in which you will construct a similar knitted texture working in the round.

Yarn

Universal Yarn Deluxe Worsted Superwash (100% superwash wool); 220 yd/200 m per 3.5 oz/100 g skein; Color: 756 Channel, 1 skein

Dimensions

7.5"/19 cm length overall, 6.5"/16.5 cm circumference (stretches to fit woman's size 9 hand)

Gauge

20 sts × 28 rows = 4"/10 cm in pattern stitch, unblocked
18 sts x 28 rows = 4"/10 cm in pattern stitch, blocked, using larger needle

Needles

US size 8/5 mm straight or circular, US size 6/4 mm 9"/23 cm circular or DPNs

Notions

Tapestry needle, stitch marker, stitch holder or 4 fabric clips

Special Stitches

Dropping and working into a stitch below: To drop down and work a stitch from a row below, gently manipulate the stitch off the left needle, undo it and the four stitches beneath it—effectively you want to work the stitch five below the one that you just came to. To do this, drop the stitch down five rows, position the left needle through this stitch in preparation to knit it. Position the left needle under the ladders so they rest on the top of the left needle to the right of the stitch you just picked up. Knit this stitch and the ladders formed, undoing the five stitches above it. It will feel awkward to do this because of the number of ladders. Manipulating the stitch and the laddered yarn formed by undoing the stitches above it together as one is how we create the textured effect. After knitting this stitch to the right needle, work another stitch, and then tighten the tension of the first two stitches on the right needle.

Page 45: Slip a pair of mitts into your pocket to have close at hand to add a pop of color, dash of style, or bit of added warmth when you take your next quiet coastal sojourn.

Pattern Notes

- Mitts are knit flat and seamed, so the circumference of the mitts can be increased or decreased to suit the desired circumference of the finished mitts by increasing or decreasing the total number of rows worked prior to beginning the decrease rows.
- Before seaming the mitts, it is advisable to try them on the hand of the intended recipient for the best fit. If not available, a "rule of thumb" measurement to use is to leave a 1.5"/4 cm gap about 1"/2.5 cm down from the top cuff for the thumb.
- Worked flat on the bias, the mitts are then seamed and the cuffs applied in the round.

INSTRUCTIONS

Using larger needle, cast on 3 sts.

Row 1 and all odd rows (WS): Sl1, purl to end of row.
Row 2 (RS): Kfb, k1, kfb. (2 sts inc)
Row 4: Kfb, k3, kfb. (2 sts inc)
Row 6: Kfb, *p1, k3, repeat from * to 3 sts from end, p1, kfb. (2 sts inc)
Row 8: Kfb, k1, *p1, k3, repeat from * until 3 sts from end, p1, k1, kfb. (2 sts inc)
Row 10: Kfb, k2, *p1, k3, repeat from * until 4 sts from end, p1, k2, kfb. (2 sts inc)
Row 12: Kfb, *k3, drop p down 5 rows, knit 5th down, repeat from * until 4 sts from end, k3, kfb. (2 sts inc)
Row 14: Kfb, *p1, k3, repeat from * to 2 sts from end of row, p1, kfb. (2 sts inc)

Repeat rows 7–14 until there are 41 sts on the needle, ending on a row 14.

Repeat row 1.

Decrease Row 1 (RS): Ssk, *p1, k3, repeat from * until last 3 sts, p1, k2tog. (2 sts dec)
Decrease Row 2 and all even rows (WS): Sl1, purl to end of row.

Decrease Row 3: Ssk, *k3, p1, repeat from * until last 5 sts, k3, k2tog. (2 sts dec)
Decrease Row 5: Ssk, k2, *drop down 5, k, k3, repeat from * until last 4 sts, drop down 5, k1, k2tog. (2 sts dec)
Decrease Row 7: Ssk, k1, *p1, k3, repeat from * until last 4 sts, p1, k1, k2tog. (2 sts dec)

Repeat decrease rows 1–8 until 7 sts remain.

Final Row: Ssk, k3, k2tog. (5 sts)

Bind off, do not cut yarn.

To facilitate holding the work in the round, with RS facing, align the cast-on and bind-off edges (see diagram on page 48), and clip together using the four fabric clips or a stitch holder.

Pick up 36 sts along one selvedge edge of the work using the 9"/23 cm circular or double-pointed US size 6/4 mm needles.

Place marker and continue in the round in a "k3, p1" fashion until the cuff is the desired length.

Bind off in pattern.

Cut yarn leaving 3"/8 cm tail.

Finishing

Using a tapestry needle, weave in ends.

Using tapestry needle and approximately 12"/30.5 cm of yarn, with RS facing, sew seam 4"/10 cm in length from the cast-on of the cuff up along the selvedge edges to join them; fasten off, weave in ends.

Leave a 1.5"/4 cm gap, sew second seam up to end of selvedge edge, approximately 1"/2.5 cm in length. Weave in ends.

Wet block; allow to air dry.

Revisit ends to make sure none revealed themselves during blocking.

Enjoy your new mitts.

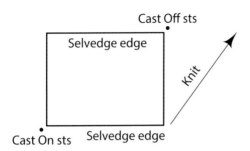

Cast Off sts

Selvedge edge

Knit

Cast On sts Selvedge edge

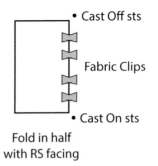

• Cast Off sts

Fabric Clips

• Cast On sts

Fold in half
with RS facing

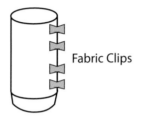

Fabric Clips

Pick up in the round
to complete cuff
using smaller needle

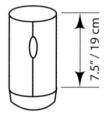

7.5" / 19 cm

Sew two seams,
leaving 1.5" / 4 cm section
unseamed for thumb hole

San Francisco Cabled Cowl

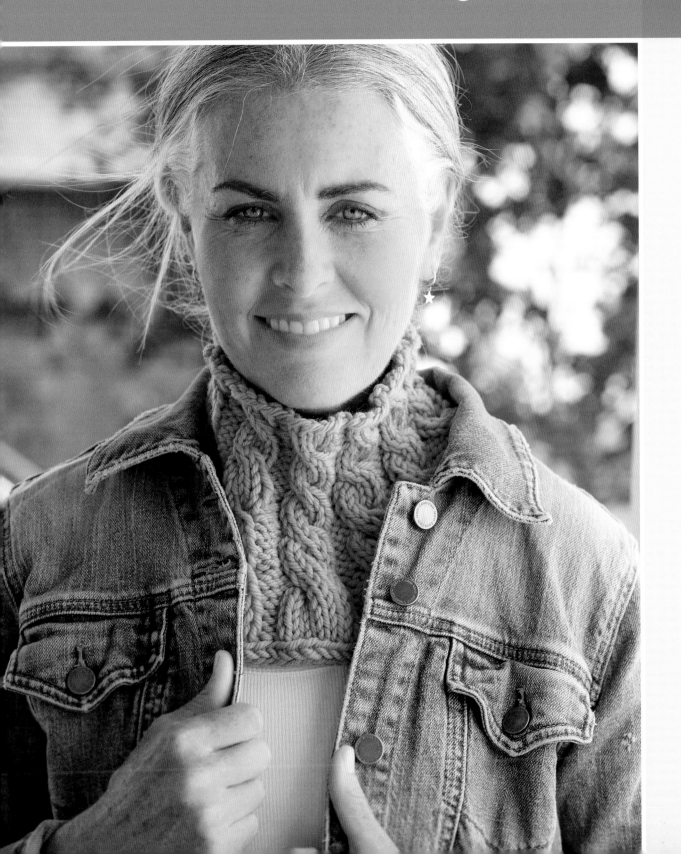

*O*ccasionally we all just need to give someone a little hug. When we cannot be there in person, it's nice to send a small gift as a token of our love. A cowl is one of my favorite items for gifting because the fit does not have to be perfect, and the color chosen need not match a coat or outfit as closely as a hat or shawl since it is not as prominent an accessory.

A cowl can be worn almost any time: around the fire pit at the beach, at home when there's just a little chill in the air, or to top off an open collar. It can also simply remind someone they are loved.

The two yarns chosen for this pattern are interesting to compare and contrast. They fall into the same weight category—#5/bulky—as they have almost the same meterage per skein and are both comprised of superwash merino wool. The effect of using one versus the other is what makes them interesting to study together.

Let's start with the Universal Yarn Deluxe Bulky Superwash. I like it because the number of plies keeps the yarn rounds, and it takes a cable well. Deluxe Bulky Superwash is spun in Turkey and commercially dyed to create consistent color through the entire skein within a given dye lot. If you are making more than one of a single color or need to make your cowl larger, make sure you have multiple skeins from the same dye lot. The yarn can be machine washed and dried—critical when gifting to someone who may not be as well versed in the fine art of knitwear care.

Pro Tip: Universal Yarn Deluxe Bulky Superwash is very easy to match to other weights in the Deluxe line, so if you do make the Seven Mile Bridge pattern (page 118) and want a cowl neck to top it off, you can use the coordinated color in Deluxe Bulky Superwash.

Cozy Color Works is hand dyed in small batches to create tonal variations which flow effortlessly throughout the entire skein. The yarn is less tightly spun than the Universal Yarn Deluxe Bulky Superwash, which gives it a lighter hand when knit, even at the same gauge. It too can be machine washed and dried; however, I personally prefer to hand wash my hand-dyed yarn collection to maintain the rich depth of color as I never really trust my washing machine to do what I can do by hand for artisanal dyed yarns. Since the yarn is dyed by hand in small batches, if you are scaling up the project or want to make more than one, be sure to check each hank of yarn for color consistency between them. For best results, lay out all the hanks untwisted side by side to see how the tonal relationships between them present. If you decide to use more than one hank to make a cowl, I suggest alternating skeins on every round and using a single hank for the I-cord bind-off should you decide on the I-cord bind-off option.

Page 49: Universal Yarn Deluxe Bulky Superwash knits up into a shipshape cowl for an uncluttered look. The cables of the San Francisco Cabled Cowl start at the top and are worked down to the shoulders, presenting the opportunity to make the piece the perfect height. Increases are hidden inside the cables so they don't distract the eye.

Yarn

Universal Yarn Deluxe Bulky Superwash (100% superwash wool); 106 yd/97 m per 3.5 oz/100 g skein; Color: 917 Summer Sky, 1 skein
or
Cozy Color Works Bulky (100% superwash merino wool); 100 yd/92 m per 3.5 oz/100 g skein; Color: Spruce, 1 skein

Dimensions

6"/15 cm high × 26"/66 cm circumference at widest point

Gauge

10 sts × 16 rows = 4"/10 cm square in stockinette stitch, worked in the round, blocked, using the larger needle

Needles

US size 10.5/6.5 mm 16"/40 cm circular needle or set of DPNs
US size 11/8 mm 16"/40 cm circular needle or set of DPNs

Notions

1 stitch marker, tapestry needle, 2 hand towels

Pattern Notes

o When adding stitches into the middle of a cable cross, the additional two stitches are added as one completes the first half of the cross. For example, C2F has two stitches held in front of the work as two stitches are worked; to add stitches between these two sets of two stitches, sl 2 to cable needle, k2, M1R, M1L, k2 from cable needle.
o Adding a purl stitch is done by purling into the back and front of a purl stitch to create a second.

A #5/bulky-weight yarn need not be cumbersome. Knit at the appropriate gauge using a creative stitch, the Universal Yarn Deluxe Bulky Superwash packs a colossal pop of color for a quick, compact project.

INSTRUCTIONS

Using smaller needle, cast on 60 sts, place marker, and join in round.

Rounds 1–5: *K4, p2, repeat from * to end of round.
Round 6: *C2F, pbf, p1, repeat from * to end of round. (10 sts inc; 70 sts)
Rounds 7–10: *K4, p3, repeat from * to end of round.
Round 11: *C2F, p3, repeat from * to end of round.

Using larger needle, continue as follows:

Rounds 12–16: *K4, p3, repeat from * to end of round.
Round 17: *Sl 2 sts to cable needle, hold cable needle in front of work, k2, M1R, M1L, k2 from cable needle, p3, repeat from * to end of round. (20 sts inc; 90 sts)

Rounds 18–22 and 24–29: *K6, p3, repeat from * to end of round.

Round 23: *C3F, p3, repeat from * to end of round.

Bind off in pattern or bind off using a three-stitch I-cord, as follows.

Three-Stitch I-Cord Bind-Off

Remove end of round marker. Using a knitted cast-on, cast on three stitches to the left needle.

Row 1: Knit 2, ssk, do not turn work, return these three stitches to the left needle.

Continue repeating row 1 until all stitches are incorporated into the I-cord.

For a tonal twist, try making the San Francisco Cabled Cowl using Cozy Color Works Bulky (bottom cowl). The tonal relationships within the yarn and the construction of the yarn give it a slightly different look and hand than the Universal Yarn Deluxe Bulky Superwash. For this version, two extra rounds were worked at the top as the hand of the yarn is softer, and the extra two rounds gave it a little more height at the chin and less at the shoulder.

Bind off remaining 3 I-cord stitches and weave in ends.

Finishing

Fill basin with warm water and a capful of your preferred delicate soap. Place cowl in the water. Do not agitate; simply press it down into the water or allow it to sink into the basin on its own as it absorbs water. Allow to sit for 20 minutes. Remove cowl from basin of water, rinse if necessary.

Place cowl on a hand towel. Place second towel over the cowl. Roll the towels together. Gently squeeze the rolled-up towels to remove excess water. Unroll the towels.

Place cowl on a dry towel or blocking mat and gently manipulate it to the desired shape. Allow the cowl to air dry.

Revisit ends to make sure none revealed themselves during washing and blocking.

Enjoy your new cowl, or wrap it up and present it to a lucky recipient.

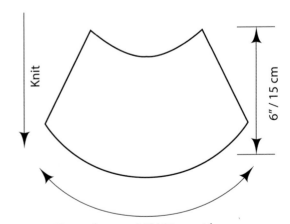

Circumference 26" / 66 cm at base,
20" / 51 cm at top

At "The End" of Long Island stands a lighthouse, high on a grassy plateau overlooking the Atlantic. On clear winter nights its outline is brightly presented against the sky with thousands of little white lights as it sits in silent vigil, warning mariners of the rocks around it. On a foggy day, the setting is not so quiet as the foghorn pierces the tranquility, warning mariners of the terrain. On a clear day you can see the outline of Block Island to the north as you paddle out to catch just the right wave.

After you're done surfing for the day, you might want a headband or cowl to add a little warmth to your outfit while the surfboard dries and you take a meditative walk along the water's edge. This convertible piece is just the perfect size for the outside pocket of your duffle. Unfurl and wear it as needed while you watch the waves crash along the shoreline.

The yarn chosen for this project was hand dyed by a fiber artist who grew up not far from the water's edge on the South Fork of Long Island. If you look closely at her yarn, you'll catch a wave or two reminiscent of a day at the beach. If you prefer a more uniform color throughout, as one would see on a lake or unusually calm day at The End, try using Deluxe Bulky Superwash available in a wide array of colors from Universal Yarn.

Yarn

Cozy Color Works Bulky (100% superwash merino wool); 100 yd/92 m per 3.5 oz/100 g skein; Color: Spruce, 1 skein

Dimensions

6¾"/17 cm high × 20"/51 cm circumference

Gauge

12 sts × 16 rows = 4"/10 cm square in stockinette stitch, blocked

Needles

US size 10.5/6.5 mm 16"/40 cm circular needle or straight needles

Notions

1 stitch marker, tapestry needle, 1 locking stitch marker, US size M/9 mm crochet hook

Optional

Spare knitting needle of similar size to hold provisionally cast-on stitches while seaming

Special Stitches

PC2B: Holding the yarn on the WS of the work, slip next two stitches to cable needle and hold these two stitches on RS of the work, p2, p2 from cable needle. When working rows featuring this stitch, you are working a WS row so it's like a "with stitches in back" p2, then p2 from cable needle.

Page 53: Worn as a headband when it's not quite cold enough for a hat, or as a pop of color to top an outfit, the undulating texture of the Montauk Waves works to hold the hair in place and frame the face for a photo-ready look.

Pattern Notes

○ For a seamless cowl, use a provisional cast-on as recommended and the Kitchener stitch to join the two ends of the cowl (see Technique Guide on pages 36–37). The additional five chain stitches in the provisional cast-on make it a bit easier to hold onto the chain itself while casting on the 15 stitches worked on the first row.

○ You may also close the loop with a three-needle bind-off (see Technique Guide); there will then be a visible seam on the right side and wrong side of the work.

○ In lieu of a provisional cast-on, you may elect to cast on using a long-tail cast-on, then cast off the last row of the work and seam along the 15 stitches to create the back seam of the cowl.

○ The pattern repeats itself every 10 rows. When increasing on each set of 10 rows, the instructions between the * * are repeated one additional time with each additional repeat of the 10 rows. For instance, when completing rows 11–20, the repeat is done three times; when these 10 rows are knitted the next time, the repeat will be done four times. This sequence may continue until you run out of yarn, in which case the pattern will morph into a shawl or poncho. The dimensions and pattern as presented were designed to maximize yarn use and minimize waste.

○ The cable cross on the purl side of the work maintains the pattern row count and symmetry. If the cables were only crossed on the right side, the effect would present in a more elongated fashion. This pattern stitch was developed to maintain the symmetry of the waves as they undulate across the fabric.

○ When slipping stitches, slip as if to purl in order to maintain an even edge. This is particularly important if you elect not to sew the three-stitch selvedge edge to the wrong side

of the work to create a hem at the top and bottom of the work.

○ A k2tog is preferred over a ssk to provide symmetry between the left and right sides of the piece when worn. If a ssk were used, the stitches would lean in the wrong direction.

○ If a wider piece with a larger circumference is desired, the number of repeats of rows 11–20 may be increased. Likewise, the number of times the decreases are done is also increased to match so the number of stitches in the cast-on and bind-off rows are the same.

When worn as a cowl, the texture of the rippled waves provides a cheery layer of warmth with minimal bulk to add just a bit of panache to your look.

INSTRUCTIONS

Using the crochet hook, chain 20. Place locking stitch marker through the last chain to prevent it from unraveling.

Cast on 15 sts using a provisional cast-on.

Setup row: Sl1, k2, p9, k3.
Row 1 (RS): Sl1, k6, p1, k4, M1L, k3. (1 st inc)
Row 2 (WS): Sl1, k3, p4, k1, p4, k3.
Row 3: Sl1, k2, *k4, p1, repeat from * twice, M1L, k3. (1 st inc)
Row 4: Sl1, k2, p1, *k1, p4, repeat from * twice, k3.
Row 5: Sl1, k2, *k4, p1, repeat from * twice, k1, M1L, k3. (1 st inc)
Row 6: Sl1, k2, p2, *k1, p4, repeat from * twice, k3.
Row 7: Sl1, k2, *k4, p1, repeat from * twice, k2, M1L, k3. (1 st inc)
Row 8: Sl1, k2, p3, *k1, p4, repeat from * twice, k3.
Row 9: Sl1, k2, *k4, p1, repeat from * twice, k3, M1L, k3. (1 st inc)
Row 10: Sl1, k2, p4, *k1, p4, repeat from * twice, k3.
Row 11: Sl1, k2, *C2F, p1, repeat from * to last 7 sts, C2F, M1L, k3. (1 st inc)
Row 12: Sl1, k2, *k1, p4, repeat from * to last 3 sts, k3.
Row 13: Sl1, k2, *k4, p1, repeat from * to last 3 sts, M1L, k3. (1 st inc)
Row 14: Sl1, k2, p1, *k1, p4, repeat from * to last 3 sts, k3.
Row 15: Sl1, k2, *k4, p1, repeat from * to last 4 sts, k1, M1L, k3. (1 st inc)
Row 16: Sl1, k2, p2, *k1, PC2B, repeat from * to last 3 sts, k3.
Row 17: Sl1, k2, *k4, p1, repeat from * to last 5 sts, k2, M1L, k3. (1 st inc)
Row 18: Sl1, k2, p3, *k1, p4, repeat from * to last 3 sts, k3.
Row 19: Sl1, k2, *k4, p1, repeat from * to last 6 sts, k3, M1L, k3. (1 st inc)
Row 20: Sl1, k2, p4, *k1, p4, repeat from * to last 3 sts, k3.
Rows 21–40: Repeat rows 11–20. (35 sts)
Row 41–44: Repeat rows 11–14. (37 sts)
Decrease Row 1 (RS): Sl1, k2, *k4, p1, repeat from * to last 4 sts, k2tog, k2. (1 st dec)
Decrease Row 2 (WS): Sl1, k2, *k1, PC2B, repeat from * to last 3 sts, k3.
Decrease Row 3: Sl1, k2, *k4, p1, repeat from * to last 8 sts, k4, k2tog, k2. (1 st dec)
Decrease Row 4: Sl1, k2, p4, *k1, p4, repeat from * to last 3 sts, k3.
Decrease Row 5: Sl1, k2, *k4, p1, repeat from * to last 7 sts, k3, k2tog, k2. (1 st dec)
Decrease Row 6: Sl1, k2, p3, *k1, p4, repeat from * to last 3 sts, k3.
Decrease Row 7: Sl1, k2, *C2F, p1, repeat from * to last 6 sts, hold 2 sts on RS of the work, knit next 2 together, knit 2 from cable needle, k2. (1 st dec)
Decrease Row 8: Sl1, k2, p2 *k1, p4, repeat from * to last 3 sts, k3.
Decrease Row 9: Sl1, k2, *k4, p1, repeat from * to last 5 sts, k2tog, k3. (1 st dec)
Decrease Row 10: Sl1, k2, p1, *k1, p4, repeat from * to last 5 sts, k3.
Decrease Rows 11–40: Repeat decrease rows 1–10. (17 sts)

Back of Cowl

Row 1 (RS): Sl1, k2, *k4, p1, repeat from * to last 4 sts, k2tog, k2. (1 st dec)
Row 2 (WS): Sl1, k2, *k1, p4, repeat from * to last 3 sts, k3.
Row 3: Sl1, k2, *k4, p1, repeat from * to last 8 sts, k4, k2tog, k2. (1 st dec)
Row 4: Sl1, k2, p4, *k1, p4, repeat from * to last 3 sts, k3. (15 sts)
Row 5: Sl1, k6, p1, k7.
Row 6: Sl1, k2, p4, k1, p4, k3.

Repeat rows 5 and 6 four additional times. Since the piece is worked sideways, the length will become the circumference when seamed; so, if the desired circumference is greater than 20"/51 cm, repeat rows

Above: Knitting with a superwash wool from side to side creates a fabric with a soft hand that is easy to wear as either a headband or a cowl. The rippled texture gives this #5/bulky-weight yarn a lighter hand than a crossed cable because there are fewer stitches crossing each other at regular intervals throughout the pattern.

A calm day that is not ideal for surfing is just perfect for a hike at The End in Montauk, New York.

5 and 6 of the Back of Cowl until the length suits the desired circumference.

Using spare needle and crochet hook if needed, remove scrap yarn from the provisional cast-on and return provisionally cast-on stitches to the spare needle.

Fold the piece in half with the WS facing to position the two sets of live stitches next to each other and begin the three-needle bind-off or Kitchener stitch along these 30 sts, 15 on each needle, to form a seam. Do not cut the yarn.

Finishing

Using the tapestry needle, weave in cast-on tail.

Using the tapestry needle and the cast-off tail, whipstitch around the selvedge edge of the cowl to secure the three-stitch garter stitch edge on the wrong side of the fabric. If the tail is quite long, cut it to approximately 2 yd/1.8 m long before using it to sew the seam.

Using a second piece of leftover yarn, whipstitch around the second selvedge edge of the cowl to secure the remaining three-stitch garter stitch edge to the wrong side of the fabric.

Steam block the finished piece. Allow it to air dry.

Revisit ends to make sure none revealed themselves during blocking.

Enjoy your new cowl.

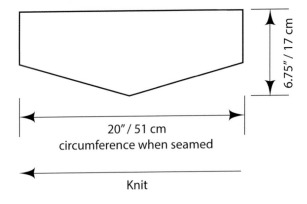

6.75" / 17 cm

20" / 51 cm
circumference when seamed

Knit

Coronado Sands Cowl

$\mathcal{T}$he inspiration for this piece comes from the cool packed sand on Coronado Island where the ocean meets the shore. It's a beautiful spot not far from downtown, worth the ferry ride to take a walk along the water's edge at low tide as the sunlight catches the sand to forge a glistening path.

After a day of cycling and swimming, the beach at the Hotel Del Coronado is one of my favorite spots to reflect and plan the evening ahead as the music flows from the hotel's piano bar through the palm trees and the firepits are set aglow. In the wintertime, as the cool breezes blow in off the Pacific, this lightweight cowl provides just enough warmth to keep me comfortable as I stroll aimlessly down the beach. When the ice rink is open, the cowl converts to a hood to keep my hair in place as I take a few laps around the rink before dinner.

Wherever your winter plans take you along the water's edge, I hope you too enjoy wearing your Coronado Sands Cowl, inspired by the sand and sea. Presented in two different yarns, one for sand and one for sea, I'd love to see where the yarn takes you on your adventures, so be sure to drop me a postcard from your corner of paradise.

Yarn

Universal Yarn Fibra Natura Cashmere Lusso (50% virgin cashmere wool, 50% recycled cashmere wool); 246 yd/225 m per 1.75 oz/50 g cake; Color: Stoppa, 2 cakes

or

Cozy Color Works Fingering (100% superwash merino); 550 yd/503 m per 3.5 oz/100 g skein; Color: Navy, 1 skein

Dimensions

19"/48 cm high × 22"/56 cm circumference

Gauge

22 sts × 24 rows = 4"/10 cm square in pattern stitch, worked in the round, blocked, using larger needle

Needles

US size 4/3.5 mm 16"/40 cm circular, US size 3/3.25 mm 16"/40 cm circular

Notions

1 stitch marker, tapestry needle

Page 59: Indulge yourself in the luxury of a hand-knit cowl to top off your look in uncluttered style.

Special Stitch

A four-stitch "k3, p1" pattern is repeated over 121 stitches in the round to present as a textured surface rather than ribbing.

Pattern Note

o The end-of-round marker is carried throughout but is ignored while maintaining the stitch pattern on the Body of the cowl. The marker is only referenced on the edge and when transitioning between the edge and body of the work.

INSTRUCTIONS

Using smaller needle, cast on 120 sts, place marker, and join in round.

Edge Stitch

Round 1: *K1, p1, repeat from * to end of round. (120 sts)

Rounds 2 and 3: Repeat round 1.

Round 4: Repeat round 1, at end of round M1L. (121 sts)

Above: For a tonal version reminiscent of the waves coming ashore, make a "sea" version using Cozy Color Works Fingering yarn in navy.

Pulled up on your head, the cowl does double duty in your wardrobe—worn here in lieu of a hat.

Body of Cowl

Transition to larger needle as you knit the setup round.

Setup Round: *K3, p1, repeat from * to last st, k1.
Round 1: Last stitch of previous round counts as first knit stitch of "k3, p1" pattern. Continue in pattern, slipping marker as you come to it, ignoring the stitch marker until work measures 18¾"/47.5 cm from cast-on edge. (121 sts)

On the last round, at the end of the round k2tog. (120 sts)

Edge Stitch

Transition to smaller needle and repeat Edge Stitch rounds 1–3.

Bind off in pattern.

Finishing

Steam block to final dimensions. Allow to air dry.

Revisit ends to make sure none revealed themselves during blocking.

Enjoy your new cowl.

With your tidy cowl around your neck, you'll never have to fuss with an oversized shawl at the farmers' market as you fill your market basket with the fixings for a farm-to-table dinner.

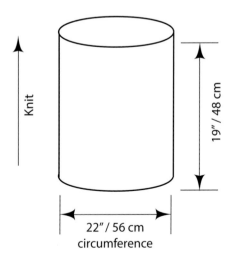

Knit

19" / 48 cm

22" / 56 cm
circumference

Key West Shrimper Hat

*T*here is a corner of Key West that few have access to without knowing exactly how to get there. From this little corner of paradise, I like to watch the sun rise over the Atlantic and set behind the horizon on the Gulf as it highlights the palm trees in the loveliest shades of sunset one can imagine. On an island where the highest elevation is a mere 12 feet, it's not difficult to find a spot to enjoy both.

As the sun rises over the horizon, the fleet of fishing boats at anchor in the shallow waters becomes visible. While the boats are too far offshore to see the shrimpers at work, I see the results of their early morning labor at the market and on the dinner table. Some mornings, believe it or not, it is a little chilly up on the roof, and I do wear a hat and gloves or mitts, especially after a morning run for croissants from Frenchie's.

In the spirit of the classic New England watch cap, with a Key West dash of color, this design has become my go-to favorite for those early mornings when I just need a little warmth as I begin my day. Not unlike the shrimpers, I like to get an early start before the island starts hopping.

Wherever you go in this hat, Pascuali Saffira will get you there in style. The yarn, available in a good range of colors as suitable for a day in Brooklyn as a morning run on Higgs Beach, has the faintest sheen to add a bit of polish to your finished hat. And, thanks to the wool, it maintains its shape season after season.

Yarn

Pascuali Saffira (75% merino ultrafine wool, 25% mulberry silk); 218 yd/200 m per 1.75 oz/50 g cake): Color 22, 1 cake

Sizes/Dimensions

Woman (Man)

Woman: 14"/36 cm around the brim, 8⅓"/22 cm from brim to crown, at rest; stretches to fit a 21"/53 cm circumference head; shown in Woman's size
Man: 18"/46 cm around brim, 9"/30 cm from brim to crown, at rest; stretches to fit 24"/61 cm circumference head

Gauge

32 sts × 36 rows = 4"/10 cm square in pattern stitch, worked in the round, unblocked, using larger needle

Needles

US size 4/3.5 mm and US size 3/3.25 mm 16"/40 cm circular needles, and US size 4/3.5 mm DPNs or two 9"/23 cm circulars for the crown

Page 63: A modern take on a slouchy hat. Comfortable to wear without the dreaded bump in the back, it looks great from every angle.

Notions

Tapestry needle, 3 markers (one to denote the end of the round and two to denote the sections for the decreases)

Pattern Notes

o   Unless otherwise indicated, slip markers as you come to them.

o   Blocking does not impact the gauge of this project due to the high silk content of the yarn.

o   Decreases are worked to the left and the right on either side of the markers as indicated. For a tidy decrease, pull the yarn a bit to tighten the stitches after each k2tog. When the work becomes too small to easily work on the US size 4/3.5 mm 16"/40 cm needle, transition it back to the shorter length needles or DPNs.

o   The hat begins with the first few rows knit flat because it can be difficult to manipulate the work into the round just after the cast-on. To make it a bit easier to join the work into the round, the fourth row is worked flat, then joined in the round and seamed with the tail from the cast-on during finishing.

o   The crown of the woman's hat will have a bit more of a curved decrease line than the man's version due to the way in which the decreases are managed versus the stitch repeat of the ribbing.

INSTRUCTIONS

Cast on 123 (138) sts using smaller circular needle using a long-tail cast-on, leaving a tail of 4"/10 cm to facilitate weaving in the ends.

Rows 1, 3 (WS): *K1, p2, repeat from * to end of row.
Row 2: *K2, p1, repeat from * to end of row.
Row 4: Repeat row 2, join in the round, pm to denote end of round.

The lightweight hand and smooth fibers that make Pascuali Saffira so attractive to knit with, worked into a timeless rib with a gently twisted crown, combine forces to give this hat the advantage of being hairstyle friendly. Slip it on and off as the winds change, and you'll be photo-ready either way.

Round 1 (RS): *K2, p1, repeat from * to end of round.
Rounds 2–6: Repeat round 1.

Transition to larger needle.

Repeat round 1 until work measures 7"/18 cm from cast-on edge.

Divide the stitches into three equal-sized sections by adding the remaining two markers at 41 (46) stitch intervals.

Woman's Decrease Round: *Knit to 4 stitches before the marker, k2togtbl, k2tog, work in pattern to next marker, repeat from *. (6 sts dec)

Man's Decrease Round: *K2tog, work in pattern to 2 sts before marker, k2togtbl, slip marker, k2tog, work in pattern to next marker, repeat from * to last 2 sts, k2togtbl. (6 sts dec)

Continue decreasing in this manner until 6 sts remain.

Cut yarn, leaving 6"/15 cm tail.

Using a tapestry needle, weave the tail back through the 6 stitches, remove them from the knitting needle(s), and draw the ring closed.

Finishing

Using tapestry needle, sew the four-row seam at the brim of the hat.

Weave in all ends.

Wash per ball band instructions and allow to air dry.

Revisit ends and weave in any that remain.

Knit

8.33 (9)" / 22 (30) cm

14 (18)" / 36 (46) cm
circumference

Above: Fishing boats out for a day's and night's work between wintry windstorms.

At right: Red sky at night, sailors' delight.

Nantucket Tradewinds Hat

The color choices for the Tradewinds Hat were selected in honor of a trip I took to Nantucket over the winter. Winter is a wonderful time to visit this island paradise—if you can take the cold. As the sea in New England takes on a darker blue/gray color, the sidewalks of Nantucket seem wider and the shell collecting more easily enjoyed along its fabled shores.

Among the many unexplained wonders of this little island—an afternoon's sail from Hyannis—is the presence of the shade of pink known as Nantucket Red, found on every manner of clothing in town. Cozy Color Works captured the tonal pink/salmon/red perfectly, reminiscent of a pair of chinos from Murray's Toggery worn while collecting scallop shells at Brandt Point fresh from the churning blue surf.

The stitch pattern, inspired by my desire to find a fresh take on the traditional knit stocking cap, is a simple four-round repeat, ideal for portable knitting wherever your travels may take you.

Yarn

Cozy Color Works Worsted (100% superwash merino wool); 200 yd/183 m per 3.5 oz/100 g skein; Color: Navy for the Child's hat, Red for the Woman's, 1 skein
Universal Yarn Deluxe Worsted Superwash (100% superwash wool); 220 yd/200 m per 3.5 oz/100 g skein; Color: 756 Channel for the Man's hat, 1 skein

Sizes/Dimensions

Child (Woman, Man)

Child: 16"/40 cm around brim, 6¾"/17 cm from brim to crown at rest; stretches to fit 21"/53 cm diameter head
Woman: 17½"/44 cm around brim, 8¼"/21 cm from brim to crown at rest; stretches to fit 22"/56 cm diameter head; shown in Woman's size
Man: 17½"/44 cm around brim, 8¾"/23 cm from brim to crown, at rest; stretches to fit 24"/61 cm diameter head

Gauge

Child: 32 sts × 30 rounds = 4"/10 cm square in pattern stitch using largest needle
Woman: 22 sts × 28 rounds = 4"/10 cm square in pattern stitch using largest needle
Man: 20 sts × 28 rounds = 4"/10 cm square in pattern stitch using largest needle
Note: Gauge is measured in the round, blocked.

Page 67: Get ready to face the day! Whether for fashion or warmth, a hat tops off the look.

Needles

Child: US size 4/3.5 mm and US size 6/4 mm 16"/40 cm circular needles, US size 5/3.75 mm DPNs

Woman: US size 6/4 mm and US size 8/5 mm 16"/40 cm circular needles, US size 7/4.5 mm DPNs

Man: US size 6/4 mm and US size 8/5 mm 16"/40 cm circular needles, US size 7/4.5 mm DPNs

Notions

4 stitch markers (one to denote end of round, three to denote quarters of the round), tapestry needle

Special Stitch

Tuck Stitch (multiple of four stitches, worked in the round with no selvedge edge):
Round 1: *K3 p1, repeat from * to end of round.
Round 2: Knit to end of round.
Round 3: Knit to end of round.
Round 4: *K3, drop down two rounds of next stitch to the purl from round 1, slip purl to left needle, push needle point under the two ladders of the dropped stitches, knit these together as one stitch, repeat from * to end of round.

Pattern Notes

○ Unless otherwise indicated, slip markers as you come to them.

○ The DPNs should be one size larger than those of the ribbing and one size smaller than those of the body to maintain the shape of the hat with minimal holes as decreases are executed in the round.

○ When working the decreases, the pattern is maintained until no purl stitches are left on the needle as decreases are done along either side of each marker, including the end of round marker.

○ Decreasing of stitches for the crown is worked on both sides of the four markers; for best results, keep these stitches tighter by pulling the yarn taut after each decrease is completed.

○ One way to remember how the pattern is maintained while decreases are done is *Knit to the knit stitch that is in the same column of stitches as the purl from round 1, drop this knit stitch down two rounds to the purl of round 1, slip purl to left needle, push needle point under the ladders of the dropped stitches, knit this stitch, repeat from * to end of round.

Pro Tip: If you make the man's hat in Deluxe Worsted Superwash, you will still have enough left over to make a pair of Oyster Creek Mitts (page 45) out of the remainder for a coordinated look that's not 100% matchy-matched.

INSTRUCTIONS

All sizes: Using a long-tail cast-on and smaller circular needle for the size desired, cast on 96 sts, join in the round, place marker to denote the end of the round, place markers every 24 sts to divide the work into four sections.

Rounds 1–16: *K3 p1, repeat from * to end of round.

Transition to larger circular needle for size desired, and continue with Tuck Stitch as follows:

Round 1: *K3 p1, repeat from * to end of round.
Rounds 2 and 3: Knit.
Round 4: *K3, drop down 2 rounds of next stitch to the purl from round 1, slip purl to left needle, push needle point under the ladders of the 2 dropped stitches, knit these together as one stitch, repeat from * to end of round.

Repeat rounds 1–4 four more times; 20 rounds completed.

Man's Hat only: Continue in pattern until work measures 7"/18 cm from cast-on edge.

All sizes:
Decrease Rounds 1 and 9: [K2tog, k1, p1, *k3 p1, repeat from * to 2 sts before m, ssk, sm] to end of round. (8 sts dec)
Decrease Rounds 2, 6, 10, 14, and 18: Knit to end of round.
Decrease Rounds 3, 7, 11, 15, and 19: [K2tog, k to 2 sts before m, ssk, sm] to end of round. (8 sts dec)
Decrease Rounds 4 and 12: *Knit to the knit stitch that is in the same column of stitches as the purl from round 1, drop this knit stitch down 2 rounds to the purl of round 1, slip purl to left needle, push needle point under the ladders of the dropped stitches, knit these together as one stitch, repeat from * to last 2 sts, k2. At the end of round 12, transition work to DPNs as round 13 is worked.
Decrease Rounds 5 and 13: [K2tog, *k3, p1, repeat from * to 2 sts before m, ssk, sm] to end of round. (8 sts dec)
Decrease Rounds 8 and 16: *Knit to the knit stitch that is in the same column of stitches as the purl from round 1, drop this knit stitch down 2 rounds to the purl of round 1, slip purl to left needle, push needle point under the ladders of the dropped stitches, knit these together as one stitch, repeat from * to end.

Child-size hat in Cozy Color Works Worsted in Navy.

Above: Tidy decreases keep the total yardage for this hat lower than expected to create a light, stylish topper.

Knit in Universal Yarn Deluxe Worsted Superwash, the textured stitches of this hat catch the light differently than the #4/ worsted-weight Cozy Color Works.

Decrease Round 17: *K2tog, k1, p1, k2, ssk, sm, repeat from * to end of round. (8 sts dec)
Decrease Round 20: *K2tog, ssk, repeat from * to end of round. (8 sts dec)

Break yarn, leaving 6"/15 cm tail.

Weave tail through remaining 8 live stitches, pull to close, fasten off, and weave in ends.

Finishing
Weave in ends.

Wash per ball band instructions.

Revisit ends to make sure none of them revealed themselves during washing and blocking. If they did, weave them back in using the tapestry needle.

Enjoy your new hat.

Optional Pom-Pom
Not all pom-poms are washable. If a pom-pom is a desired add-on, it is best to attach it using a button rather than attaching it directly to the hat itself so it can be removed when fashion changes or the hat needs to be washed. The method below requires a button of sufficient size to allow the tails of the pom-pom to pass through the button's holes or shank.

To add a pom-pom, using a tapestry needle and with the wrong side of the hat facing you, feed the tails of the pom-pom through the top of the hat. Align the shank or holes of a button to the tails of the pom-pom. Pull the tails through the button. Using the tapestry needle, pass each tail through the button shank or holes a few times, and make a bow out of the tails of the pom-pom and the tail of the hat's yarn tail rather than a knot so the pom-pom can be removed and reattached or swapped out as desired.

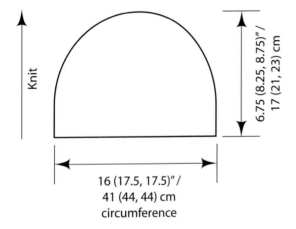

Knit

6.75 (8.25, 8.75)" / 17 (21, 23) cm

16 (17.5, 17.5)" / 41 (44, 44) cm circumference

Nauset Beach Bandana

Have you ever picked up a yarn that creates an immediate sense of happiness from deep in your memory? For me, Universal Yarn Fibra Natura Ravello is one of those yarns. The moment I picked it up, the Sea Whisper colorway reminded me of happy times spent at Lighthouse Beach looking east toward Nauset Beach as the waves crashed behind it, the sun bathing the horizon in shades of white, sand, sky, and sea on early morning strolls. Knit into this bandana, it becomes the perfect summer layer.

Ravello is one of my favorite yarns because it truly transitions throughout the seasons, regardless of the port in which you may find yourself. The cotton keeps it wearable throughout the seasons as a little pop of color with a simple pair of jeans and a tank, while the thoughtful additions of wool and cashmere provide the cotton the structure it needs to keep it light and retain its shape.

For a slightly larger bandana, Universal Yarn Wool Pop makes a wonderful version of the Nauset Beach Bandana, knitting up at a slightly heavier 23 sts × 30 rows. Shown in Graphite, color 607, it reminds me of my bluestone path at home that leads to the hydrangea cutting garden. The wingspan of the Wool Pop Nauset Beach Bandana is 48"/122 cm, and the depth is 21"/53 cm.

As with many patterns in this collection, the repeat can be repeated as many times as you like to create a longer or shorter version of the piece, and the yarn weight can be changed as well. I made a series of these using hand-dyed #4/worsted-weight yarn as holiday gifts. For reference, 200 yd/183 m of #4/worsted-weight yarn on a US size 8/5 mm needle will produce a scarf with a 42"/107 cm wingspan and 16"/40 cm depth at a gauge of 18 sts × 28 rows.

That precious skein of yarn you picked up on your last vacation or that favorite leftover one from a big project deserves to be adorning an outfit and not at the bottom of your knitting bag, so go get it and make a triangle bandana for yourself or as a quick-to-knit gift. Got a few skeins? Knit away and let the finished size be determined by your yardage. Enjoy the journey.

Pro Tip: Given the nature of a yarn featuring this amount of cotton, it is recommended that you use bamboo or driftwood needles rather than metal as the latter may not provide a sufficient amount of tension between the yarn and needle as you work from corner to corner on the bias.

Page 73: Just the right size to wear under a jacket without the extra bulk of a shawl, this bandana provides a graceful layer of warmth on a chilly spring morning.

Yarn

Universal Yarn Fibra Natura Ravello (75% cotton, 16% extra fine merino wool, 9% recycled cashmere); 207 yd/190 m per 1.75 oz/50 g cake; Color: 109 Sea Whisper, 1 cake

Needle

US size 5/3.75 mm 24"/61 cm circular needle

Notions

Tapestry needle, row counter, blocking board, blocking wires, blocking pins

Gauge

24 sts × 32 rows = 4"/10 cm square in stockinette stitch, unblocked

Dimensions

37.5"/95 cm wingspan, 16"/40 cm at deepest point, unblocked; sides measure 37.5"/95 cm, 27"/69 cm, and 22"/56 cm, unblocked; 42"/107 cm wingspan, 17"/43 cm, blocked

INSTRUCTIONS

Cast on 3 sts.

Row 1 (RS): Kfb, k to end of row. (1 st inc)
Row 2 and all even rows through 52 (WS): Sl1wyif, purl to end of row.
Rows 3–14: Repeat rows 1 and 2. (10 sts)
Row 15: Kfb, yo, k2togtbl, k7. (11 sts)
Row 17: Kfb, k2, yo, k2togtbl, k6. (12 sts)
Row 19: Kfb, k4, yo, k2togtbl, k5. (13 sts)
Row 21: Kfb, k6, yo, k2togtbl, k4. (14 sts)
Row 23: Kfb, k8, yo, k2togtbl, k3. (15 sts)
Row 25: Kfb, yo, k2togtbl, k8, yo, k2togtbl, k2. (16 sts)
Row 27: Kfb, k2, yo, k2togtbl, k8, yo, k2togtbl, k1. (17 sts)
Row 29: Kfb, k4, yo, k2togtbl, k8, yo, k2togtbl. (18 sts)

The ease with which Ravello knits means that you'll be done with this bandana in no time and looking forward to making another.

Row 31: Kfb, k6, yo, k2togtbl, k9. (19 sts)
Row 33: Kfb, k8, yo, k2togtbl, k8. (20 sts)
Row 35: Kfb, *yo, k2togtbl, k8, repeat from * until 9 sts remain, yo, k2togtbl, k7. (1 st inc)
Row 37: Kfb, k2, *yo, k2togtbl, k8, repeat from * until 8 sts remain, yo, k2togtbl, k6. (1 st inc)
Row 39: Kfb, k4, *yo, k2togtbl, k8, repeat from * until 7 sts remain, yo, k2togtbl, k5. (1 st inc)
Row 41: Kfb, k6, *yo, k2togtbl, k8, repeat from * until 6 sts remain, yo, k2togtbl, k4. (1 st inc)
Row 43: Kfb, k8, *yo, k2togtbl, k8, repeat from *until 5 sts remain, yo, k2togtbl, k3. (1 st inc)
Row 45: Kfb, *yo, k2togtbl, k8, repeat from * until 4 sts remain, yo, k2togtbl, k2. (1 st inc)
Row 47: Kfb, k2, *yo, k2togtbl, k8, repeat from * until 3 sts remain, yo, k2togtbl, k1. (1 st inc)

Above: For days when you just don't feel like a necklace and want a little something to break up a T-shirt and jeans outfit, this bandana is light enough to wear as a colorful accessory.

Wool Pop and Ravello are shown side by side to show the slight difference in the two fabrics. The eyelet pattern makes the difference in gauge negligible after blocking the two.

Row 49: Kfb, k4, *yo, k2togtbl, k8, repeat from * until 2 sts remain, yo, k2togtbl. (1 st inc)

Row 51: Kfb, k6, *yo, k2togtbl, k8, repeat from * until 11 sts remain, yo, k2togtbl, k9. (1 st inc)

Row 53: Kfb, k8, *yo, k2togtbl, k8, repeat from * to end of row. (1 st inc)

Repeat rows 35–54 until yarn is almost depleted. When three times the amount needed to complete a row remains, bind off purlwise having just finished a RS row. Approximately 100 sts will be on the needle if the suggested yarn is used.

Finishing

Weave in ends, wet block, and allow to air dry.

Revisit ends to make sure none revealed themselves during washing and blocking.

Enjoy your new bandana.

Pro Tip: While not necessary, the use of blocking wires is recommended to facilitate blocking out the piece after knitting.

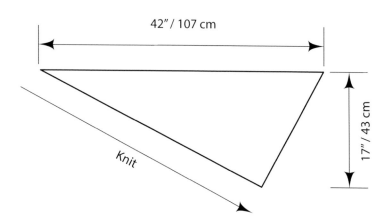

42" / 107 cm

17" / 43 cm

Knit

F ar from the crowds and T-shirt shops on Duval Street just off Higgs Beach is one of the prettiest little spots in the Florida Keys, West Martello Tower. Originally designed as a coastal fortification used during the U.S. Civil War, it now protects the Key West Garden Club's collection of plants. Here among the vaulted brick spaces and local fauna you can take in the view, learn about local history, and simply reflect on the many different textures and colors that envelop the space. The colors of this shawl are reminiscent of my favorite part of the landscaping here—the orchids. If you visit, don't forget to look up into the trees; there are wonders to behold at all levels from the ground up at the West Martello Tower.

The rhythm of the color in English Garden, worked into columns of stockinette, is the key to this shawl. The dynamic composition of the colors within English Garden encourages the eye to explore it. When substitutions are made, choose yarn based on the cadence of the color to achieve similar results.

Yarn

Cozy Color Works Worsted (100% superwash merino wool); 200 yd/183 m per 3.5 oz/100 g skein; Color: English Garden, 2 skeins

Dimensions

65"/165 cm wingspan, 25"/63 cm deep at widest point

Gauge

18 sts × 22 rows = 4"/10 cm square in stockinette stitch, blocked

Needles

US size 8/5 mm 24"/61 cm circular needle, and second of same or one size smaller to facilitate dropping stitches

Notions

Tapestry needle

Optional

Blocking pins, board, wires

When the forecast calls for a chilly day at the mouth of the bay, add a layer of warmth over your go-to turtleneck and jeans.

Pattern Notes

o Knit on the bias, this shawl grows from 5 to 125 sts.

o Gauge is not vital to the success of the project.

o The ladders between the columns of stockinette are formed by dropping the middle purl stitch of the purled set in the "k5, p3" rib.

o Rows 26, 28, 30, 32, 34, 36, and 38 state the number of times to repeat between the * for the rows is twice; however, when repeating this series of even rows, the number of times the repeat is done will increase by one each time the pattern is repeated. For example, the second time you work these rows, the repeat will be done three times rather than twice.

o After dropping the center purls back to the point at which they were cast on, when picking up stitch between the two remaining purls, you may elect to use a backwards loop cast-on or, using the left needle, pick up the bar between the two remaining purls and knit that stitch through the back of the loop. The former is a bit loose, the latter is tighter—try both on your swatch to see which you prefer.

INSTRUCTIONS

Cast on 5 sts.

Setup row: Purl.
Row 1 (RS): Kfb, k4. (6 sts)
Row 2 (WS): Sl3wyif, pm, p3.
Row 3: Kfb, knit to end of row. (1 st inc)
Row 4: Sl3wyif, purl to end of row.
Rows 5–10: Repeat rows 3–4. (10 sts)
Row 11: Kfb, yo, p1, k to end of row. (2 sts inc; 12 sts)
Row 12: Sl3wyif, purl to 4 sts from end, k1, p3.
Row 13: Kfb, p3, knit to end of row. (13 sts)
Row 14: Sl3wyif, p5, k3, purl to end of row.
Row 15: Kfb, k1, p3, knit to end of row. (14 sts)
Rows 16, 18, 20, 22, and 24: Sl3wyif, p5, k3, purl to end of row.

The asymmetrical shape of this shawl lends itself well to wearing it in different ways. There is no "wrong way" to wear it—the only wrong thing to do would be to let it languish in the closet.

Row 17: Kfb, k2, p3, knit to end of row. (15 sts)
Row 19: Kfb, k3, p3, knit to end of row. (16 sts)
Row 21: Kfb, k4, p3, knit to end of row. (17 sts)
Row 23: Kfb, k5, p3, knit to end of row. (18 sts; there are now 7 sts at the beginning of the row)
Row 25: Kfb, yo, p1, *k5, p3, repeat from * until 8 sts remain, knit to end of row. (2 sts inc)
Rows 26, 28, 30, 32, 34, 36, and 38: Sl3wyif, *p5, k3, repeat from * twice (see Pattern Notes), purl to end of row.
Row 27: Kfb, *p3, k5, repeat from * to 3 sts from end, k3. (1 st inc)
Row 29: Kfb, k1, *p3, k5, repeat from * to 3 sts from end, k3. (1 st inc)
Row 31: Kfb, k2, *p3, k5, repeat from * to 3 sts from end, k3. (1 st inc)

Row 33: Kfb, k3, *p3, k5, repeat from * to 3 sts from end, k3. (1 st inc)
Row 35: Kfb, k4, *p3, k5, repeat from * to 3 sts from end, k3. (1 st inc)
Row 37: Kfb, k5, *p3, k5, repeat from * to 3 sts from end, k3. (1 st inc; there are now 7 sts at the beginning of the row)

Repeat rows 25–38 as presented and increase the number of times the *p5, k3* repeat is done on even rows by one for each repeat until there are a total of 122 sts on the needle.

Continue in pattern for an additional three rows working the stockinette stitches as follows: On the RS the "k5" is replaced with "k2, p1, k2," and on the WS the "p5" is replaced with "p2, k1, p2" to maintain the appearance of the columns while at the same time creating a ribbed edge to counteract the natural inclination of knitted fabric to roll along the cast-off edge. (125 sts)

See Pattern Notes.

Transition the work to a second circular needle; as you do this, drop the middle purl of each p3 ridge down to the point at which it was cast on. The stitch that was dropped from the needle will present as a horizontal bar between the two purl stitches that remain on the needles. After dropping the middle purl stitch, using the tip of the right needle, cast on one stitch using the top bar of the dropped stitch to maintain the stitch count. (125 sts)

Bind off all sts. Suggested bind-off: k2tog through the back of the loop, pass stitch to right needle, then pass back to left to bind off, and k2tog with next stitch on the left needle.

Finishing
Wash per ball band instructions.

Block wet; straighten out the columns of dropped stitches as you position the shawl on the blocking surface.

Allow to dry.

Revisit ends to make sure none revealed themselves during blocking. If they did, use the tapestry needle to weave them in.

Enjoy your new shawl.

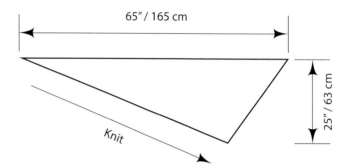

The colors of English Garden are reminiscent of a piece of impressionist art from the mid-nineteenth century. Short lines of color create a brilliant composition across the field of stockinette columns.

East Bay Coastline Shawl

The coastline is not static. It is alive with motion, just like this shawl. It moves with you like the waves quietly fluttering to shore on a calm day, creating pockets of color and shadow. Soft and subtle, the yarn itself evokes a sense of calm and is perfectly paired with a simple repeat to flow effortlessly from cast-on to bind-off. Think of this pattern as a blank canvas on which your chosen yarn will paint a story, evoke a memory, and make someone smile. Wear it as a sarong for quick trips to the beach bar or as a shawl. Wherever it may take you, it will take you there with a sense of effortless elegance. I keep one in the basket on the front of my bike. It's just the right weight for late afternoon trips down the East Bay Bicycle Trail to my local yarn store in Barrington, Rhode Island, on long, lazy July days when it is just a little too windy to take out the stand-up paddleboard for a bit of exercise. If you're out there too, I'm easy to find—just look for the bike with Otto the Happy Hound running alongside it or snoozing on the front of my board.

Yarn

Darn Good Yarn Lace Weight Silk (100% recycled silk); 300 yd/275 m per 1.75 oz/50 g skein; Color: Caribbean, 3 skeins

Dimensions

96"/244 cm wingspan, 42"/107 cm deep at widest point

Gauge

24 sts × 24 rows = 4"/10 cm square in stockinette stitch, blocked

Needles

US size 8/5 mm 24"/61 cm circular needle, second of same or one size smaller to facilitate dropping stitches

Notions

Tapestry needle, blocking pins, blocking board, blocking wires

The negative space formed by the dropped purl stitches between the columns of stockinette promotes movement of the piece as it catches the breeze while you move through your day.

Pattern Notes

- Knit on the bias, this shawl grows from 5 to 205 stitches.
- Gauge is not vital to the success of the project.
- The ladders are formed by dropping the middle purl stitch of the purled set in the "k5, p3" rib.
- Rows 26, 28, 30, 32, 34, 36, and 38 state the number of times to repeat between the * for the rows is twice; however, when repeating this series of even rows, the number of times the repeat is done will increase by one each time the pattern is repeated. For example, the second time you work these rows, the repeat will be done three times rather than twice.

- After dropping the middle purls back to the point at which they were cast on, when picking up stitch between the two remaining purls, you may elect to use a backwards loop cast-on or, using the left needle, pick up the bar between the two remaining purls and knit that stitch through the back of the loop. The former is a bit loose, the latter is tighter—try both on your swatch to see which you prefer.
- When dropping the purl stitch, take care not to tear the silk roving yarn. To reduce the chance of tearing it, a crochet hook or blunt tapestry needle may be helpful to coerce stuck stitches.

Embrace the beauty of the bay, or simply the memory of it, as you wrap this shawl around yourself.

INSTRUCTIONS

Cast on 5 sts.

Setup row: Purl. (5 sts)
Row 1 (RS): Kfb, k4. (6 sts)
Row 2 (WS): Sl1wyif, k2, p3.
Row 3: Kfb, knit to end of row. (1 st inc)
Row 4: Sl1wyif, k2, purl to end of row.
Rows 5–10: Repeat rows 3–4. (10 sts)
Row 11: Kfb, yo, p1, knit to end of row. (2 sts inc; 12 sts)
Row 12: Sl1wyif, k2, p to 4 sts from end, k1, p3.
Row 13: Kfb, p3, knit to end of row. (13 sts)
Row 14: Sl1wyif, k2, p5, k3, purl to end of row.
Row 15: Kfb, k1, p3, knit to end of row. (14 sts)
Rows 16, 18, 20, 22, and 24: Sl1wyif, k2, p5, k3, purl to end of row.
Row 17: Kfb, k2, p3, knit to end of row. (15 sts)
Row 19: Kfb, k3, p3, knit to end of row. (16 sts)
Row 21: Kfb, k4, p3, knit to end of row. (17 sts)
Row 23: Kfb, k5, p3, knit to end of row. (18 sts; there are now 7 sts at the beginning of the row)
Row 25: Kfb, yo, p1, *k5, p3, repeat from * until 8 sts remain, knit to end of row. (2 sts inc)
Rows 26, 28, 30, 32, 34, 36, and 38: Sl1wyif, k2, *p5, k3, repeat from * twice (see Pattern Notes), purl to end of row.
Row 27: Kfb, *p3, k5, repeat from * to 3 sts from end, k3. (1 st inc)
Row 29: Kfb, k1, *p3, k5, repeat from * to 3 sts from end, k3. (1 st inc)
Row 31: Kfb, k2, *p3, k5, repeat from * to 3 sts from end, k3. (1 st inc)
Row 33: Kfb, k3, *p3, k5, repeat from * to 3 sts from end, k3. (1 st inc)
Row 35: Kfb, k4, *p3, k5, repeat from * to 3 sts from end, k3. (1 st inc)
Row 37: Kfb, k5, *p3, k5, repeat from * to 3 sts from end, k3. (1 st inc; there are now 7 sts at the beginning of the row)

Repeat rows 25–38 as presented and increase the number of times the *p5, k3* repeat is done on even

The playful way in which the dye dances across the silk yarn gives every skein its own personality, taking center stage on a simple field of stockinette.

rows by one for each repeat until there are a total of 202 sts on the needle.

Continue in pattern an additional 3 rows, working the stockinette sts as follows: On the RS the "k5" is replaced with "k2, p1, k2," and on the WS the "p5" is replaced with "p2, k1, p2" to maintain the appearance of the columns while at the same time creating a ribbed edge to counteract the natural inclination of knitted fabric to roll along the cast-off edge. (205 sts)

Transition the work to a second circular needle; as you do this, drop the middle purl of each p3 ridge down to the point at which it was cast on. The stitch that was dropped from the needle will present as a horizontal bar between the two purl stitches, which remain on the needles. After dropping the middle purl stitch, using the tip of the right needle, cast on one stitch using the top bar of the dropped stitch to maintain the stitch count. (205 sts)

Bind off all sts. Suggested bind-off: k2tog through the back of the loop, pass stitch to right needle, then pass back to left to bind off, and k2tog with next stitch on the left needle.

Finishing

Steam block, using blocking wires to maintain straight edges and open the columns of dropped stitches. Allow to dry naturally.

Revisit ends to make sure none revealed themselves during blocking. If they did, use the tapestry needle to weave them in.

Enjoy your new shawl.

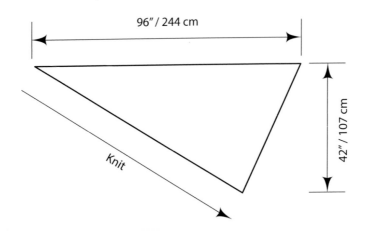

The subtle texture of the recycled silk fibers in this yarn helps it stay in place as you go about your day, collecting seashells by the seashore or wherever your agenda takes you.

Cold Spring Harbor Hooded Shawl

There is a small inlet near the Cold Spring Harbor Fish Hatchery on the north shore of Long Island, which is one of my favorite spots to sit by the water's edge and read on a winter day. With a delicious slice of chocolate chip pie on the picnic table and a cup of coffee from Sweetie Pies on Main, I can always catch a refreshing break from the toils of modern life, knitting in hand right here. If your travels cross mine, feel free to bring your project bag along and join me for a few rows over a cup. At this time of the year it's helpful to have a hood, thus the reason I created this version of my striped shawl, coupling a self-striping yarn with a superwash DK. This version is more compact than the Ocean Beach Sunset Poncho (page 93), just the right size to roll up and tuck behind the seat of my roadster and yes, before you ask, I do drive it with the top down year-round—makes it easier to spot in any parking lot.

Yarn

MC: Universal Yarn Fibra Natura Dona (100% extra-fine merino superwash); 126 yd/115 m per 1.75 oz/50 g cake; Color: 120 Heritage Day, 6 cakes

CC: Universal Yarn Colorburst (65% superwash merino wool, 35% acrylic); 660 yd/600 m per 7 oz/200 g ball; Color: 106 Earth and Sky, 1 ball

Dimensions

70"/178 cm wingspan × 34"/86 cm at deepest point, hood 10"/22.5 cm deep × 26"/66 cm along seam

Gauge

18 sts × 28 rows = 4"/10 cm square in stockinette stitch using Dona, blocked

Needle

US size 8/5 mm 30"/76 cm circular needle

Notions

Tapestry needle, 4 locking stitch markers, blocking board, blocking pins

Pattern Notes

o   The hooded shawl is worked in two separate pieces, which are joined during the finishing process.

o   For a refresher on how to work Kitchener stitch, see the Technique Guide on page 36.

o   If you are stash busting or cannot get enough of a single MC, make the hood first, then make the shawl as large as you can with the available yarn.

o   When "stash busting" a project like this, divide the available yarn by the quantity you have of each, then decide how best to arrange the striping. Keep in mind that the piece will grow from the top along the center spine out toward the edges, so the final few rows will use a great deal more yarn than the first few rows.

Page 87: The hood on this shawl was not an applied afterthought. It was created as part of the piece so that it can be easily styled by tucking it behind the shawl when not in use.

- To reduce the need to look at the pattern on every row, use different-colored markers: two of color A to indicate M1L and two of color B to indicate M1R.
- Slip markers as you come to them on WS rows, working increases only on the right side as described.
- Hood is worked flat, the cast-on edge becomes the brim which frames the face when worn, and the live stitches on the last row become the back of the hood when seamed.

INSTRUCTIONS

Shawl

Using MC, cast on 5 sts.

Row 1 (WS): K2, pm (color A), k1, pm (color B), k2.

Row 2 (RS): K2, pm (color A), M1L, sm (color B), k1, sm (color A), M1R, pm (color B), k2. (2 sts inc)

Row 3 and all WS rows unless specified: K2, purl to 2 sts from end of row, k2.

Row 4 (RS): K2, sm, M1L, knit to m, M1R, sm, k1, sm, M1L, knit to m, M1R, sm, k2. (4 sts inc)

Rows 5–20: Repeat rows 3–4. (43 sts)

Row 21: Repeat row 3. Cut MC, leaving 4"/10 cm tail.

Rows 22 and 26: Using CC, repeat row 4.

Rows 23 and 25: Repeat row 3.

Row 24: K2, sm, (yo, k2tog) to 1 st from m, yo, k1, yo, sm, k1, sm, yo, k1, (yo, ssk) to m, yo, sm, k2. (4 sts inc)

Cut CC, leaving 4"/10 cm tail.

Rows 27–46: Using MC, repeat rows 3 and 4.

Row 47: Repeat row 3.

Cut MC, leaving 4"/10 cm tail.

Rows 48–52: Using CC, repeat rows 22–26.

Repeat rows 27–52 three more times for a total of five stripes of MC and five of CC.

Repeat rows 27–46 once more.

When deployed, the hood provides a layer of warmth. The elastic nature of the way in which Dona is spun helps keep your hair in place so that when you arrive at your destination, the hood that helped protect you from the elements is not a hindrance to your look.

Final Contrasting Color Stripe

Row 1 (WS): Using CC, k2, purl to 2 sts from end of row, k2.

Row 2 (RS): K2, sm, M1L, knit to m, M1R, sm, k1, sm, M1L, knit to m, M1R, sm, k2. (4 sts inc)

Row 3: K2, sm, yo, *p2tog, yo, repeat from * to 1 st from m, p1, yo, sm, p1, sm, yo, p1, **yo, p2tog, repeat from ** to m, yo, sm, k2. (4 sts inc)

Row 4: Repeat row 2.

Rows 5 and 6: Knit.

Using the same pattern on the hood and shawl itself provides the opportunity for the two to work together while letting the long self-striping runs of color in Colorburst take center stage.

Below: The clever way in which Dona is spun gives it incredible drape as it works with the Colorburst. Styled with the hood up or down, there is no bad angle on this versatile accessory.

Cast off using a stretchy bind-off. As shown, the bind-off was done as k1, *pass st back to left needle, k2togtbl, repeat from * to end of row.

Fasten off.

Hood

Using CC, cast on 120 sts, pm between 60th and 61st sts.

Rows 1–5: Sl1, knit to end of row.
Row 6 (WS): Using MC, sl1, purl to end of row.
Row 7: Sl1, knit to end of row.
Rows 8–25: Repeat rows 6 and 7.
Row 26: Repeat row 6. Cut MC, leaving 4"/10 cm tail.
Row 27: Using CC, sl1, knit to end of row.
Row 28: Sl1, purl to end of row.
Row 29: Sl1, (yo, k2tog) to 1 st from m, k1, sm, k1, (yo, ssk) to last st, k1.
Row 30: Repeat row 28.
Row 31: Repeat row 27. Cut CC, leaving 4"/10 cm tail.
Rows 32–51: Using MC, repeat rows 6 and 7. Cut MC, leaving 4"/10 cm tail after row 5

Repeat rows 27–51 one additional time.

With RS facing, leave stitches on the needle.

Fold the Hood along the live edge of stitches, using the marker to help you see where the halfway point is located; there will be 60 stitches on each side of the circular needle.

Using the Kitchener stitch, work along the 120 live stitches to seam them.

Finishing

Steam block the two panels to the stated dimensions. Pin to blocking board and allow the pieces to air dry. Remove the pins from the pieces.

With the WS facing, place the Shawl in front of you with the deepest point closest to you and the longest side the farthest away from you.

With the WS facing, position the Hood's selvedge edge along the middle of the longest side of the shawl. The Kitchener seam of the Hood should align to the middle of the initial five stitches that were cast on for the shawl. Pin the selvedge edge of the Hood to the top edge of the Shawl, aligning the MC and CC stripes to each other as you pin the Hood into place.

Using the mattress stitch, join the two pieces along this seam.

Steam the finished object to settle the seam into place.

Revisit ends to make sure none revealed themselves during blocking. If they did, use the tapestry needle to weave them in.

Enjoy your new hooded shawl.

For a different look, swap the yarn and colorways used for the main color and contrasting color, and add in a second contrasting color for additional visual interest. The Color-burst itself is the star of this piece as it undulates from color to color in wide, lazy stripes, interrupted only by the lacy rows done in a solid color for additional visual impact.

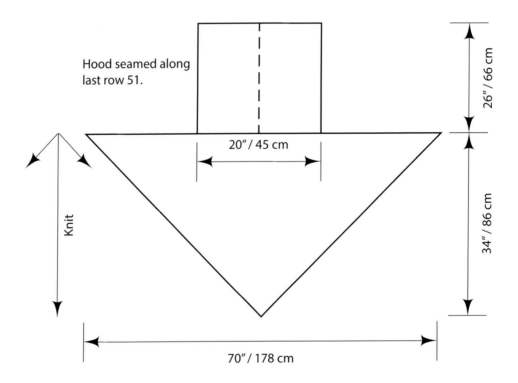

Hood seamed along last row 51.

Knit

20" / 45 cm

26" / 66 cm

34" / 86 cm

70" / 178 cm

Ocean Beach Sunset Shawl/Poncho

This poncho was born out of the popularity of shawls. My knitting group was talking about how tough it is to wear a shawl in a new and innovative way. Sure, a rectangle can become a shrug or cocoon, but collectively we were stumped by what could be done with a triangle. So, with that in mind, I set out to make a piece of wearable fiber art as simple to make as a shawl while also being easy to just pop on after a workout or over a sundress for entertaining friends for morning coffee. The result: a poncho fashioned out of my most popular shawl pattern with a few little lacy bits to keep it interesting. You'll enjoy working it with a big ball of cheery colors between fields of "knitmeditation" stockinette.

Named for the sweet spot at the end of Newport Avenue right on Ocean Beach where surfers gather all year round, this poncho will serve you all year round, too. Whether you're stopping through for a burger at Hodad's or noodles at OB's, do yourself a favor—time the trip so you can catch the sunset right on the beach. Prefer your sunsets a little more serene? Wander onto the Ocean Beach Pier and, as you enjoy the energy of the setting sun, listen to the waves and take it all in. Prefer an active pursuit, perhaps less active than partaking of the surfing? Pick up the Sunset Cliffs Coastal trail along the water's edge just south of the pier.

Yarn

MC: Universal Yarn Deluxe DK Superwash (100% superwash wool); 284 yd/259 m per 3.5 oz/100 g ball; Color: 819 Purplish Blue, 4 balls
CC: Universal Yarn Colorburst (65% superwash merino wool, 35% acrylic); 660 yd/600 m per 7 oz/200 g ball; Color: 114 Sunset, 1 ball

Dimensions

70"/178 cm wingspan × 29"/74 cm depth at deepest point, wet blocked

Gauge

20 sts and 24 rows = 4"/10 cm square in stockinette stitch using MC, unblocked

Needle

US size 8/5 mm 30"/76 cm circular needle

Notions

Tapestry needle, 4 locking stitch markers, fabric clips, blocking wires, blocking board, blocking pins, 2 large colorfast beach towels

Pattern Notes

o To reduce the need to look at the pattern on every row, use different-colored markers: two to indicate M1L and two to indicate M1R.
o Slip markers as you come to them on WS rows.

Page 93: On the windward side of the porch as the morning sun frames the view, be connected to the moment and reflect on the beautiful sunset the evening before as you greet the new day.

- Love the look but prefer a shawl? Just make one instead of two panels. There's no one stopping you. Unwind, sit back, and enjoy a glass of sauvignon blanc as you watch the sunset over your favorite bay.
- For a shawl, I recommend cutting colors as you switch between them, leaving 4"/10 cm tails which are woven in after blocking.
- The nature of superwash wool is to stretch when wet. This allows for the piece to be stretched to an ample size with a 70"/178 cm wingspan and 29"/74 cm depth at the widest point. If washed and dried per ball band instructions, the piece will be tighter and smaller, closer to a 66"/168 cm wingspan and 27"/69 cm depth.

INSTRUCTIONS

Shawl Panel (Make 2)

Using MC, cast on 5 sts.

Row 1 (WS): P2, pm, p1, pm, p2.
Row 2 (RS): K2, pm, M1L, sm, k1, sm, M1R, pm, k2. (2 sts inc)
Row 3 and all WS rows unless specified: Purl all sts.
Row 4 (RS): K2, sm, M1L, knit to m, M1R, sm, k1, sm, M1L, knit to m, M1R, sm, k2. (4 sts inc)
Rows 5–20: Repeat rows 3 and 4. (43 sts)
Row 21: Using CC, repeat row 3.
Rows 22 and 30: Repeat row 4. (47 sts)
Rows 23, 25, 27, and 29: Repeat row 3.
Rows 24 and 28: K2, M1L, *yo, k2tog, repeat from * to 1 st from m, yo, k1, sm, k1, sm, k1, *yo, ssk, repeat from * to m, yo, M1R, sm, k2. (4 sts inc)
Row 26: K2, M1L, *yo, k2, pass yo over 2 sts, repeat from * to 1 st before m, yo, k1, M1R, pass yo over 2 sts, sm, k1, sm, yo, M1L, k1, pass yo over 2 sts, *yo, k2, pass yo over 2 sts, repeat from * to m, M1R, sm, k2.
Rows 31–46: Using MC, repeat rows 3 and 4.

The beauty of this piece is in the details. Starting the Colorburst stripes from the same spot in the color repeat provides alignment of the stripes (shown here at the shoulder), matching each other stitch for stitch as they work their way down to the wrist. The use of a simple mattress stitch seam lets the eye rest on the colors rather than the seam itself. For a more bohemian look, add a faux crochet seam atop it and fringe the edges.

Rows 47–56: Using CC, repeat rows 21–30.

Continue in this fashion working rows 31–56, until six stripes of MC and five of CC have been completed.

Final Stripe

Using CC:

Rows 1, 3, 5 and 7 (WS): Purl.
Row 2 (RS): K2, sm, M1L, knit to m, M1R, sm, k1, sm, M1L, knit to m, M1R, sm, k2. (4 sts inc)

Row 4: K2, M1L, *yo, k2tog, repeat from * to 1 st from m, yo, k1, sm, k1, sm, k1, *yo, ssk, repeat from * to m, yo, M1R, sm, k2. (4 sts inc)

Rows 6, 8, 9 and 10: Knit.

Bind off all stitches using a stretchy bind-off.

Finishing

Using tapestry needle, weave in ends.

Allow pieces to settle into a sink full of warm water, approximately 110° F, and sit for 20 minutes. Add hand-washing soap and gently work the pieces to clean and relax them.

From all angles this poncho presents an undulating cascade of color like the sun dancing across the water, effortlessly bathing the shoreline. It reveals cheerful bursts of colorful stripes in sync with your every move.

Below: In those few golden moments as a series of brilliant colors radiate along the sky in the early morning and late afternoon, one simply must reflect on the beauty of everyday life and the wonders of nature during Mother Nature's Happy Hour. Colorburst in the colorway Sunset is just the right blend of tonal relationships to mimic the beauty of the setting sun on a shimmering sea, bringing with it the promise of another day well spent and one to follow.

Remove the pieces one at a time from the water and allow them to drain for 10 minutes.

Spread out a colorfast beach towel on the floor or counter. Place first piece on the beach towel. Gently roll the piece up in the beach towel. Squeeze the towel to remove moisture from the piece. Unfurl the beach towel, remove the piece.

Using a second towel, repeat this process on the second piece.

Using blocking boards or a suitable blocking surface, lay the pieces out to dry, gently blocking them to the finished dimensions.

When the pieces are dry, align them with RS facing each other.

Along the top of the work, the longest side of the triangle, measure off the middle 10"/25.5 cm and mark with stitch markers.

Place one sewing clip approximately every 4"/10 cm from the corners to the stitch markers, aligning the two pieces to facilitate seaming.

Using MC and tapestry needle, beginning at one corner, sew using a mattress stitch along the two selvedge edges. When you get to the first stitch marker, remove the marker and sew into the same stitch several times to secure the edge. Weave in the end and cut the tail.

Repeat for second shoulder.

Revisit ends to make sure none revealed themselves during blocking. If they did, use the tapestry needle to weave them in.

Enjoy your new poncho.

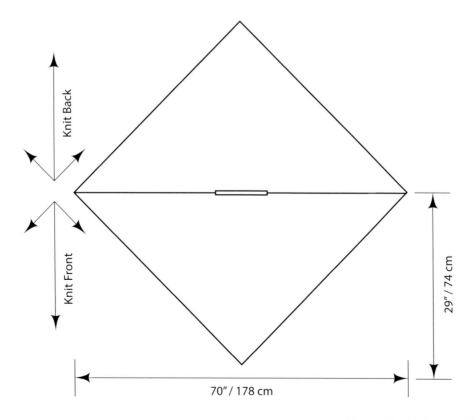

70" / 178 cm

29" / 74 cm

Knit Back

Knit Front

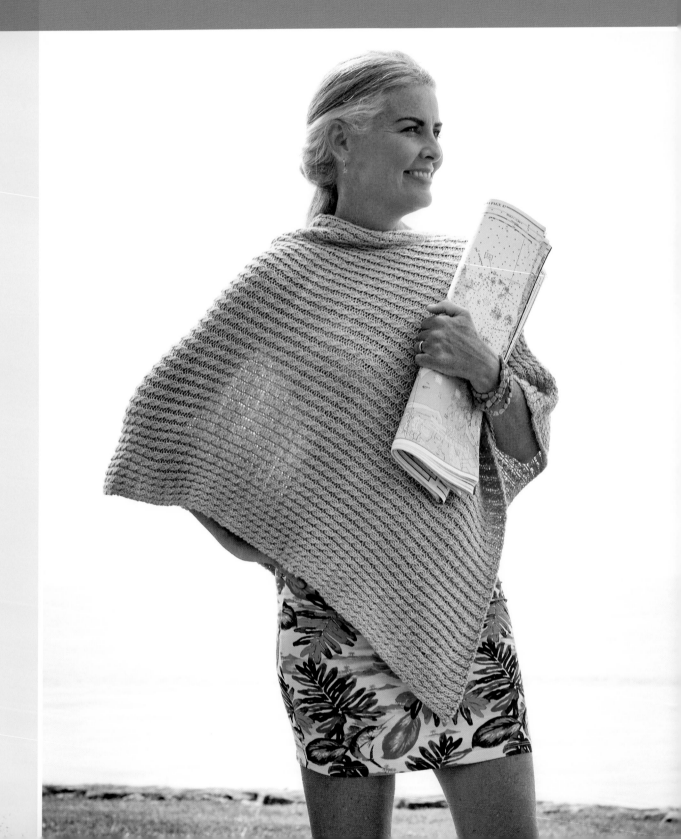

From coast to coast, a poncho is a perfect accessory for layering. Dress it up, dress it down—the possibilities are endless for integrating it seamlessly into your wardrobe. Elevate the everyday by adding one or two to your wardrobe.

The color of this yarn reminds me of the color of the water I splash through in the early morning hours of long, lazy winter days in the Florida Keys. This particular poncho is my go-to for early morning walks in January when I have a few moments to savor the sunshine just after the sun rises. It is warm enough to cut that early chill on Simonton Street when I pick up my coffee at the Cuban Coffee Queen or enjoy a bite at Sunset at the Pier House with friends. On those rare days when the mercury does not climb above 70° F, it pulls double duty as a sit-upon as I enjoy my lunch from Letitia's Food Truck on Higgs Beach.

Knit in a superwash wool, the Atlantic Poncho is a little heavier than its Pacific counterpart (page 103), for those days when you cannot count on the jet stream or sun reflecting off the sand.

Yarn

Cozy Color Works DK (100% superwash merino); 275 yd/251 m per 3.5 oz/100 g skein; Color: Sea Spray, 4 (4, 5) skeins

Sizes

Finished to fit bust sizes 34 (40, 48)"/86 (101, 122) cm

Finished Dimensions, folded and seamed

25 (28, 31)" long × 26 (29, 32)" wide/64 (71, 79) cm long × 66 (74, 81) cm wide (see schematic; shown in size 34"/86 cm)

Gauge

20 sts × 28 rows = 4"/10 cm square in pattern stitch before blocking; 19 sts × 24 rows = 4"/10 cm square in pattern stitch after blocking

Needle

US size 6/4 mm 24"/61 cm circular needle (Addi Turbo Rocket Squared recommended to cable without a cable needle and retain tension)

Notions

Tapestry needle, point protectors, blocking wires, blocking board, blocking pins

Special Stitch

A trompe l'oeil faux cable created using a "k2, p1" stitch repeat with a crossover every fourth row formed by knitting through the back of the second stitch on the left needle, then knitting the first stitch on the left needle before dropping both and proceeding to the purl.

The cabled stitch of the Atlantic Poncho provides the perfect backdrop for a hand-dyed artisanal yarn to take top billing wherever the charts may take you.

Pattern Notes

o The gauge of superwash wool is particularly relevant when blocking, as the number of plies, density of the twist, and length of the fibers each play a role in how the yarn will respond to the blocking process. Cozy Color Works worked in a cabled pattern retains its shape when blocked and worn. Other yarns may yield different results; therefore, be mindful of your gauge swatch before and after blocking before casting on.

o The suggested yarn, Cozy Color Works DK, is a superwash wool. Superwash wool tends to stretch when worn so rather than fight it, this pattern takes advantage it and is wet blocked prior to final seaming.

o Given the artisanal nature of the Cozy Color Works collection, there are no dye lots. Therefore, when purchasing the yarn, purchase a sufficient amount to complete the project and work from two skeins at a time to minimize any variation from hank to hank. To keep the yarn from tangling, work each ball from its own yarn bowl or bag.

o This poncho is knit as a rectangle from side to side, blocked, folded in half, then seamed along the shoulder.

o To customize the fit from shoulder to waist, cast on more stitches for a longer poncho, fewer for a shorter poncho.

o To customize the fit from shoulder to shoulder, knit additional rows in groups of four to maintain pattern consistently from beginning to end for a wider finished garment. Knit fewer rows in groups of four to create a narrower version. When adjusting the fit from shoulder to shoulder, maintain a 12"/30.5 cm neck opening for ease of pulling the poncho over your head.

INSTRUCTIONS

Cast on 121 (139, 157) sts.

Row 1 (RS): Sl1 as if to purl, *k2, p1, repeat from * to end of row.

Row 2 (WS): Sl1 as if to purl, *p2, k1, repeat from * to end of row.

Row 3: Sl1 as if to purl, *knit into back of the second st on the left needle, do not drop it or the first st on the left needle, knit the first st on the left needle, drop both sts off the left needle (2 knit sts now on the right needle), p1, repeat from * to end of row.

Row 4: Repeat row 2.

Repeat rows 1–4 until work measures approximately 51 (57, 63)"/130 (145, 160) cm, having just completed a row 4.

Repeat rows 1–2.

Bind off using a stretchy bind-off.

Finishing

Weave in ends.

Blocking is accomplished by rolling up the fabric loosely and resting it in a sink of warm water at 110° F.

Remove the garment from the sink, unroll it, and place it between two bath towels. Beginning at one edge, roll the three layers and squeeze the rolled-up set of three layers to release some of the water.

Block the rectangle to 25 (28, 31)" × 52 (58, 64)"/64 (71, 79) cm × 132 (148, 162) cm.

When the rectangle is dry, with the WS facing, fold the left side over the right. The RS is now facing, and the garment is folded to appear as it would when worn. To seam, turn the piece inside out. With WS facing, graft the shoulder stitches together using a mattress stitch. Working from the cast-on edge

The light hand of a subtle #3/DK-weight yarn makes this poncho a wardrobe staple for multiple seasons. It can be coupled with a sundress as shown, or worn as an extra layer under a winter coat. The key to it is the yarn—a thicker yarn would be too bulky to do dual duty.

The twist of Cozy Color Works DK gives the cables definition while providing the elasticity needed for the poncho to drape gracefully over the person lucky enough to wear it.

corner of the fabric, begin to sew the seam along the top of the rectangle. Suggested seam length 14 (17, 20)"/36 (43, 50) cm will result in a neck opening of approximately 12"/30 cm.

Revisit ends to make sure none revealed themselves during blocking. If they did, use the tapestry needle to weave them in.

Enjoy your new poncho.

The smooth fibers of superwash wool make the DK-weight Cozy Color Works a comfortable choice for this lightweight poncho.

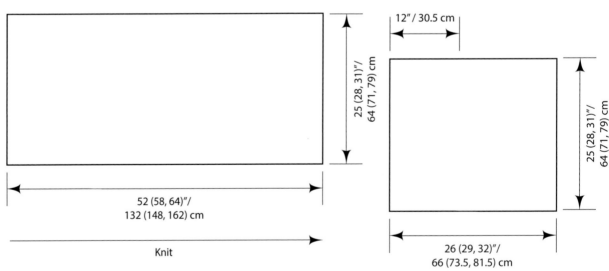

25 (28, 31)"/
64 (71, 79) cm

52 (58, 64)"/
132 (148, 162) cm

Knit

12" / 30.5 cm

25 (28, 31)"/
64 (71, 79) cm

26 (29, 32)"/
66 (73.5, 81.5) cm

Pacific Poncho

You know that perfect morning when you get up early and have the whole beach to yourself for a nice, long walk? Just you, a cup of coffee in your own mug, and—if they are lucky—your significant other and dog. This is the poncho to put on over your cami or T-shirt to give you a bit of coverage while you wait for the heat of the sun to warm you. On the flip side of the day, it's perfect for a fireside chat or walk under the stars. The subtle shimmer of the rayon and metallic fibers that make up this incredibly soft yarn will capture the dawn's early light as well as the light of the moon or flame from the firepit. Like the Santa Monica Shell (page 137), this poncho was inspired by the ease with which the yarn can be stitched into a fine, shimmering piece of wearable art, as lovely as the twinkle of the lights from shore shining out over the sea.

Yarn

Blue Heron Rayon Metallic (85% rayon, 15% metallic); 550 yd/502 m per 8 oz/227 g skein; Color: Carnelian, 2 (2, 3) skeins

Sizes

Finished to fit bust sizes 34 (40, 48)"/86 (102, 122) cm

Finished Dimensions, folded and seamed

25 (28, 32)″ × 29 (33, 37)″/63 (71, 81) cm × 74 (84, 94) cm (see schematic; shown in size 34″/86 cm)

Gauge

28 sts × 28 rows = 4"/10 cm square in pattern stitch, unblocked
21 sts × 26 rows = 4"/10 cm square in pattern stitch, blocked

Needle

US size 5/3.75 mm 24"/61 cm circular needle (bamboo is recommended to maintain gauge given the silky hand of this yarn)

Notions

Tapestry needle, point protectors, blocking wires, blocking board, blocking pins

Special Stitch

A trompe-l'oeil faux cable is created using a "k2, p1" stitch repeat with a crossover every fourth row, formed by knitting through the back of the second stitch on the left needle, then knitting the first stitch on the left needle before sliding the two new stitches to the right needle and proceeding to the purl.

Page 103: Perfect for weekend entertaining at the summer house or relaxing on the beach midweek, the Pacific Poncho will set the tone for relaxed elegance.

Pattern Notes

- This poncho is knit as a rectangle, blocked, folded in half, then seamed along the shoulder.
- The nature of this stitch creates a dense fabric, which is given a lighter hand by blocking the piece prior to seaming the shoulder.
- The suggested rayon yarn, Blue Heron Rayon Metallic, when knit in the suggested stitch stretches when worn. To minimize the impact of this when wearing the garment, the piece is knit to smaller dimensions, then wet blocked to the appropriate size. It will continue to stretch when worn; the dimension along the cast-on and bind-off rows will likely become approximately 25"/63.5 cm after it is worn a few times, approximately 3"/8 cm wider than blocked. It can be reblocked to make it more dense. If you want a smaller size, you may also choose to knit at a tighter gauge.
- When rolling Blue Heron Rayon Metallic into a ball, it is suggested that you do not use a yarn swift or make a center-pull ball. Enlist the help of a willing accomplice to make a ball with you or put the hank over the backs of two chairs. This yarn is best made into a ball from which the yarn is pulled from the outside. Once it is made into a ball, store each ball in its own zip-top bag to prevent it from unrolling. When knitting, knit from the bag for the same reason.

INSTRUCTIONS

Cast on 121 (139, 157) sts.

Row 1 (RS): Sl1 as if to purl, *k2, p1, repeat from * to end of row.

Row 2 (WS): Sl1 as if to purl, *p2, k1, repeat from * to end of row.

Row 3: Sl1 as if to purl, *knit into back of the second st on the left needle; do not drop it or the first st on the left needle; knit the first st on the left needle, drop both off the left needle (two knit sts now on the right needle), p1, repeat from * to end of row.

Row 4: Repeat row 2.

Repeat rows 1–4 until work measures approximately 51 (59, 67)"/130 (150, 170) cm from cast-on edge, having just completed a row 4.

Repeat rows 1–2.

Bind off using a stretchy bind-off.

Chic need not be fussy or difficult to achieve.

Above: The hassle-free grace of Blue Heron Rayon Metallic sets the tone for a level of refinement unmatched by other yarns. Worked from side to side, the restrained colorway presents as a field of vertical stripes to enhance the finished poncho as it works with the columns of graceful cables.

Savor that special moment in time just as the sun starts to rise, kissing the boardwalk with a gentle glow, illuminating the sand as the palm trees start to sing, awakened by the warm breeze flowing ashore.

Finishing

Weave in ends.

Blocking is accomplished by rolling up the fabric loosely and resting it in a sink of warm water at 110° F. There may be some color loss depending on the temperature of the water. Add one cup white vinegar if there is any color loss. When the garment sinks into the basin, allow it to sit for approximately 20 minutes; do not agitate the water.

If vinegar was used, rinse the fabric.

Remove the garment from the sink, unroll it, and place it between two bath towels. Beginning at one edge, roll the three layers and squeeze the rolled-up set of three layers to release some of the water.

Block the rectangle to 22 (25, 29)″ × 58 (66, 74)″/56 (64, 74) cm × 148 (168, 188) cm. When the rectangle is dry, with the WS facing, fold the left side over the right. The RS is now facing, and the garment is folded to appear as it would when worn. To seam, turn the piece inside out. With WS facing, graft the shoulder stitches together. Working from the cast-on edge corner of the fabric, begin to sew

the seam along the top of the rectangle, leaving a neck opening of approximately 12″/30.5 cm (see diagram).

Revisit ends to make sure none revealed themselves during blocking. If they did, use the tapestry needle to weave them in.

Enjoy your new poncho.

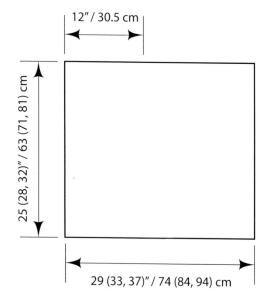

12″ / 30.5 cm

25 (28, 32)″ / 63 (71, 81) cm

29 (33, 37)″ / 74 (84, 94) cm

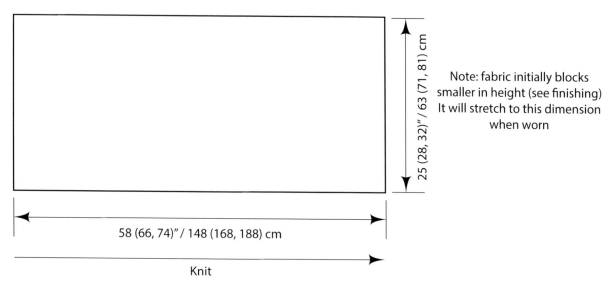

25 (28, 32)″ / 63 (71, 81) cm

Note: fabric initially blocks smaller in height (see finishing) It will stretch to this dimension when worn

58 (66, 74)″ / 148 (168, 188) cm

Knit

Newport Clambake Poncho

Have you ever noticed the color variation of the water as you motor or sail from port to port along the East Coast? The rich aquas, teals, and royal blues of the Gulf, with a gentle breeze flowing, the white caps frothing over the deep blues . . . the green, almost brownish/silver tones off Maine . . . it's hard to believe it's the same water.

In my travels from shop to shop along the coast, sometimes a particular hand-dyed yarn will simply jump off the shelf at me to bring back a flood of aquatic memories. This was the case the first time I laid eyes upon the deep tonal blues in Cozy Color Works Navy and Deep Sea Blue. Although only a short bike ride from the fabled sailing waters of Long Island Sound made famous by F. Scott Fitzgerald's *The Great Gatsby*, these colors took me further north into colder Gilded Age–steeped waters in Narragansett Bay, to a little cove we frequent just outside Newport. It's a great location for a clambake, and thus the name of this poncho, Newport Clambake. When the breezes start to kick up in the bay, it will keep you comfortable in quintessential seaside style as you gather around the firepit to enjoy the fruits of your day spent clamming, crabbing, and fishing.

Yarn

Cozy Color Works Fingering (100% superwash merino); 550 yd/503 m per 3.5 oz/100 g skein; MC: Navy, 2 (3) skeins; CC: Deep Sea Blue, 1 skein

Dimensions

40 (48)"/102 (124) cm wide × 21"/53 cm long at shoulder; shown in smaller size

Gauge

24 sts × 30 rows = 4"/10 cm square in stockinette stitch, unblocked

Needle

US size 7/4.5 mm, 24"/61 cm circular needle

Notions

Tapestry needle, 8 plastic locking stitch markers to denote edges of neck and corresponding point along the hem, blocking board, knit blockers

Pattern Notes

o   Poncho is worked from side to side, flat with shaping on only one selvedge edge; the other selvedge edge remains a three-stitch I-cord formed by slipping the first three stitches on every WS row.

o   While similar to the Intracoastal Sunrise Poncho (page 114), the nature of the two yarns—both the same weight but with a different twist and slightly different compositions—produces two fabrics of different gauges and final dimensions. The Cozy Color Works has a bit more structure to retain a closer ratio between its blocked and unblocked gauge.

Lightweight yarn creates a diaphanous layer for your seaside look.

- The neckline is formed by shaping along the selvedge edge on RS rows, while at the same time slipping the first three stitches with the yarn held on the WS of the work. On neckline rows without shaping, the first three stitches on the RS row are slipped to maintain the same rolled edge as on the bottom hem.
- The plastic locking stitch markers, placed at the neckline, will facilitate seaming the pieces during finishing. **Plastic is recommended as metal locking markers may rust when the pieces are blocked and stain the fabric. Please do not remove them when blocking the pieces prior to seaming.**
- To make a wider version, increase the number of rows worked on either side of the neckline shaping.
- To make a longer version, cast on more stitches.
- To make a wider neck opening, increase the number of rows between the neck shaping sections.
- Any changes made to the front must also be made on the back to maintain the symmetry of the finished piece.
- Colorwork striping as presented in the sample assumes that the knitter will be making one of the two stated sizes. If a larger or smaller width is desired, it is suggested that the width be adjusted at the garment's full length (in sections where there are 120 stitches on the needle rather than between individual rows of increases or decreases), as changing the number of rows worked when increasing or decreasing will impact the shaping.

Colorwork Striping

Front: Color blocks are worked from the cast-on edge as follows: Use MC until the point at which the shoulder decreases for the second shoulder are worked, approximately 30 (38)"/76 (97) cm from the cast-on edge. Change to CC and work an additional 5"/13 cm. Change to MC and work

an additional 3"/8 cm; change to CC and repeat this stripe. Change to MC and work an additional 1.5"/4 cm; change to CC and repeat this stripe, less four rows; knit four rows in CC. In order to maintain the color striping along the front and back when the pieces are joined, the color repeats are worked in the reverse on the back from the cast-on edge.

Back: Color blocks are worked from the cast-on edge as follows: Work in CC 1.5"/4 cm, change over to the MC and work an additional 1.5"/4 cm, change to the CC and work 3"/8 cm, switch to the MC and work a second 3"/8 cm stripe in the MC, continue for an additional 5"/13 cm in CC, then work the remaining rows of the back in the MC, including the 15 repeats to form the shoulder panel between the cast-on edge and the neckline shaping.

Styled with the shoulder seams off the shoulder, the poncho presents itself differently—two looks from one.

INSTRUCTIONS

Note: Do not remove markers until pieces are assembled. The markers aid in the placement of the two pieces atop each other to maintain a graceful transition around the neck.

Front

Cast-on to Neckline:

Using MC, cast on 110 sts.

Knit 4 rows.

Row 1 (RS): Sl1, k1, M1R, knit to end of row.
Row 2 (WS): Sl3, purl to end of row.
Rows 3, 5, and 7: Sl1, knit to end of row.
Rows 4, 6, and 8: Sl3, purl to end of row.

Repeat rows 1–8 a total of 10 times. (120 sts)

Repeat rows 3 and 4 an additional 7 (15) times; work measures approximately 14 (18)"/36 (46) cm from cast-on edge, ending with a WS row.

Neckline to second shoulder:

Place plastic locking stitch markers on selvedge edges to denote first row of neckline decreases.

Decrease Row 1 (RS): Sl1, k1, k2tog, knit to end of row. (1 st dec)
Decrease Row 2 (WS): Sl3, purl until 2 sts remain, p2tog. (1 st dec)

Repeat decrease rows 1 and 2 a total of five times. (110 sts)

Continue in stockinette, slipping the first 3 sts on RS and WS rows with no additional shaping, until work measures 24.5 (28.5)"/62 (72) cm from cast-on edge.

Increase Row 1 (RS): Sl1, k1, M1R, knit to end of row. (1 st inc)
Increase Row 2 (WS): Sl3, purl to 1 st before end of row, M1p, p1. (1 st inc)

Repeat increase rows 1 and 2 a total of five times. (120 sts)

Knitting side to side makes the vertical colorwork easy—no intarsia or extra twisting, just a blissfully easy set of ends to weave in later.

Place locking plastic stitch markers on selvedge edges to denote the end of the increase rows having just finished a WS row. (120 sts)

Larger size only: Continue in pattern using MC, with no additional increases or decreases until work measures 32.5"/82.5 cm from cast-on edge.

Second shoulder to bind-off (see Pattern Notes regarding colorwork)

Using CC to begin and MC as indicated in the Pattern Notes, continue as follows:

Row 1 (RS): Sl1, knit to end of row. (120 sts)
Row 2 (WS): Sl3, purl to end of row.

Repeat rows 1 and 2 a total of seven times.

Paired with a coordinated tank, the poncho looks more like a top than a topper.

Begin decreases as follows, creating striping as described in the Pattern Notes for Front:

Row 1 (RS): Sl1, k1, k2tog, knit to end of row. (1 st dec)

Row 2 (WS): Sl3, purl to end of row.

Rows 3, 5, and 7: Sl1, knit to end of row.

Rows 4, 6, and 8: Sl3, purl to end of row.

Repeat rows 1–8 a total of 10 times. (110 sts)

Using CC, knit 4 rows.

Bind off.

Back

Cast-on to Neckline

Using CC, cast on 110 sts (see Pattern Notes and change colors as described for the Back)

Knit 4 rows.

Changing colors as described in the Pattern Notes, continue as follows:

Row 1 (RS): Sl1, k1, M1R, knit to end of row. (1 st inc)

Row 2: Sl3, purl to end of row.

Rows 3, 5, and 7: Sl1, knit to end of row.
Rows 4, 6, and 8: Sl3, purl to end of row.

Repeat rows 1–8 a total of 10 times. (120 sts)

Repeat rows 3 and 4 an additional 7 (15) times until work measures 14 (18)"/36 (46) cm from cast-on, ending with a WS row.

Neckline to Second Shoulder
Using MC, continue as follows:

Place plastic locking stitch markers on selvedge edges to denote first row of neckline decreases.

Decrease Row 1 (RS): Sl1, k1, k2tog, k to end of row. (1 st dec)
Decrease Row 2 (WS): Sl3, purl until 2 sts remain, p2tog. (1 st dec)

Repeat decrease rows 1 and 2 a total of five times. (110 sts)

Continue in stockinette, slipping the first 3 sts on RS and WS rows with no additional shaping, until work measures 24.5 (28.5)"/62 (72) cm from cast-on edge; end having just completed a WS row.

Increase Row 1 (RS): Sl1, k1, M1R, knit to end of row. (1 st inc)
Increase Row 2 (WS): Sl3, purl to 1 st before end of row, M1p, p1. (1 st inc)

Repeat Increase Rows 1 and 2 a total of five times. (120 sts)

Place locking stitch markers on selvedge edges to denote the end of the increase rows, having just finished a WS row.

Larger size only: Continue in pattern, with no additional increases or decreases until work measures 32.5"/82.5 cm from cast-on edge.

Second Shoulder to Bind-off
All sizes: Using MC, continue as follows:

Row 1 (RS): Sl1, knit to end of row. (120 sts)
Row 2 (WS): Sl3, purl to end of row.

Repeat rows 1 and 2 a total of seven times.

Decrease Row 1 (RS): Sl1, k1, k2tog, knit to end of row. (1 st dec)
Decrease Row 2 (WS): Sl3, purl to end of row.
Decrease Rows 3, 5, and 7: Sl1, knit to end of row.
Decrease Row 4, 6, and 8: Sl3, purl to end of row.

Repeat decrease rows 1–8 a total of 10 times. (110 sts)

Knit 4 rows.

Bind off.

Finishing
Lightly block to suit preferred hand and dimensions.

With RS facing each other, align neck markers. Using preferred seaming method, seam along shoulders. Remove markers.

Steam to desired final dimensions.

Revisit ends to make sure none revealed themselves during blocking. If they did, use the tapestry needle to weave them in.

Enjoy your new poncho.

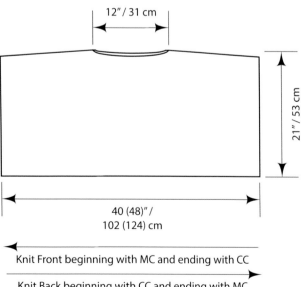

12" / 31 cm

21" / 53 cm

40 (48)" / 102 (124) cm

Knit Front beginning with MC and ending with CC

Knit Back beginning with CC and ending with MC

Intracoastal Sunrise Poncho

S ock yarn too pretty to wear on your feet? I agree! There are a lot of beautiful self-striping and self-patterning sock yarns available. So rather than stick with the pedestrian design constraint that sock yarn is just for socks, here it is elevated and celebrated as a poncho. Wear this poncho over a tank in the summer, with a turtleneck in the transitionary seasons, and as an extra layer under a coat in the depths of a long, cold winter. The light hand makes it easy to gather at the neck as a toasty warm layer under a coat. I use mine as a cuddly Shavasana layer at the end of yoga class.

The colors of Alanya Sock Love Letter remind me of the deep tonal relationships along the horizon when the sun begins to rise on the Intracoastal Waterway near Palm Beach, Florida.

Yarn

Darn Good Yarn Indigo Quail Alanya Sock Yarn (75% merino wool, 25% nylon); 130 yd/119 m per 1 oz/30 g cake; Color: 005 Love Letter, 10 cakes

Needle

US size 7/4.5 mm 24"/61 cm circular needle

Notions

Tapestry needle, 8 plastic locking stitch markers to denote edges of neck and corresponding positions on the bottom hem, blocking board, knit blockers

Gauge

22 sts × 28 rows = 4"/10 cm square in stockinette stitch, unblocked

Dimensions

44"/112 cm wide × 23"/58 cm at shoulder, blocked (see schematic)

Bold, bright, and beautiful.

Pattern Notes

- When picking out your yarn, think about how you may wear your piece. For the most flexible care, use a superwash wool or wool/nylon blend sock yarn. The added durability of #1/sock-weight yarn versus #1/fingering-weight or #0/lace-weight yarn will make the piece more stable, wash after wash. To create the same vertical striping as presented in the sample, use the indicated cakes of self-striping sock yarn from the inside and outside of the cake as directed. Other matched cakes of sock yarn will produce similar results; the key is to pull from the inside and outside of the cakes as directed to create the bookmarked stripes.
- When working the rows, take care to use one cake from the outside, then the second cake from the inside, alternating inside/outside as each cake is worked, to create the striping effect shown in the sample. For smaller color blocks, always pull from the same point in the cake or use a variety of cakes from different colorways.
- Poncho is worked flat with shaping on only one selvedge edge, while the other remains a three-stitch I-cord formed by slipping the first three stitches on every WS row.

- The neckline is formed by shaping along the selvedge edge on RS rows, while at the same time slipping the first three stitches with the yarn held on the WS of the work. On rows without shaping, the first three stitches on the RS row are slipped to maintain the same rolled edge as on the bottom hem.
- The neckline and hem markers on the selvedge edges will facilitate seaming the pieces during finishing. Please do not remove them when blocking the pieces prior to assembly. The markers on the hem help keep the front and back straight when seaming along the shoulder. The nylon in this yarn makes it a bit more slick with which to work.
- To make a wider version, increase the number of rows worked on either side of the

Self-striping sock yarn, pulled from opposite ends of the cakes on the front and back, is used to create mirrored stripes.

neckline shaping. Each cake of Alanya will create approximately 7″/18 cm of width on the poncho.
- To make a longer version, cast on more stitches.
- To make a wider neck opening, increase the number of stitches between the neck shaping sections.

INSTRUCTIONS
Front
Cast on 110 sts.

Knit 4 rows.

Side Edge to First Shoulder
Row 1 (RS): Sl1, k1, M1R, knit to end of row. (1 st inc)
Row 2 (WS): Sl3, purl to end of row.
Rows 3, 5, and 7: Sl1, knit to end of row.
Rows 4, 6, and 8: Sl 3, purl to end of row.

Repeat rows 1–8 a total of 10 times. (120 sts)

Repeat rows 3 and 4 an additional seven times.

Neckline
Place plastic locking stitch markers along the selvedge edges of the work to denote the first row of neckline decreases.

Decrease Row 1 (RS): Sl1, k1, k2tog, knit to end of row. (1 st dec)
Decrease Row 2 (WS): Sl3, purl until 2 sts remain, p2tog. (1 st dec)

Repeat decrease rows 1 and 2 a total of five times. (110 sts)

Continue in stockinette, slipping the first 3 sts on RS and WS rows with no additional shaping, until work measures 21″/53.5 cm from the cast-on edge.

Increase Row 1 (RS): Sl1, k1, M1R, knit to end of row. (1 st inc)

Increase Row 2 (WS): Sl3, purl to 1 st before end of row, M1p, p1. (1 st inc)

Repeat increase rows 1 and 2 a total of five times. (120 sts)

Second Shoulder to Bind-off

Place plastic locking markers on selvedge edges at beginning of first RS row to denote where the shoulder begins and neckline ends.

Decrease Row 1 (RS): Sl1, k1, k2tog, knit to end of row. (1 st dec)
Decrease Row 2 (WS): Sl3, purl to end of row.
Decrease Rows 3, 5, and 7: Sl1, knit to end of row.
Decrease Rows 4, 6, and 8: Sl3, purl to end of row.

Repeat decrease rows 1–8 a total of 10 times. (110 sts)

Knit 4 rows.

Bind off.

Back

Work as for Front. Begin with opposite end of the first yarn cake and work as for Front until there are 120 sts on the needle (see Pattern Notes).

Shape neckline using ssk rather than k2tog to maintain the mirrored angles of the decreases between the front and back panels.

Finishing

Lightly block to suit preferred hand and dimensions.

With RS facing each other, align neck markers.

Using preferred seaming method, seam along shoulders.

Revisit ends to make sure none revealed themselves during blocking. If they did, use the tapestry needle to weave them in.

Enjoy your new poncho.

Slipping stitches at the same spot of each row creates an even edge as the neckline is shaped.

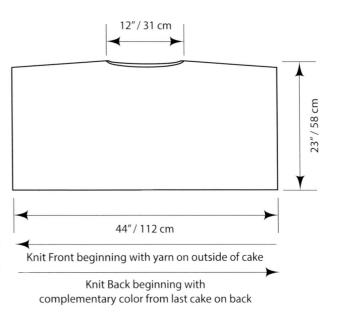

12" / 31 cm

23" / 58 cm

44" / 112 cm

Knit Front beginning with yarn on outside of cake

Knit Back beginning with complementary color from last cake on back

Seven Mile Bridge Poncho

Driving along the Overseas Highway from Key Largo to Key West, you cannot help but marvel at the serenity of the teal blue water on both sides of Route 1 and the palm trees as they gently sway in the breeze. Sometimes it takes a lot of imagination to filter out the roadside commerce, but once you hit the Seven Mile Bridge, you are enveloped by the tranquility of the water on both sides of the roadway.

If you're driving, this is the perfect time to take a break and walk out to Pigeon Key on the section of the old bridge, get a grouper sandwich over at the Sunset Grille and Raw Bar, or venture off the beaten path that is the Overseas Highway and stop in at the Keys Fisheries for the peel-and-eat shrimp. Email me—I'll send you the directions to this hidden gem.

If you're fortunate enough to be the passenger in the car, take it all in: Knight Key Channel, the small old buildings still standing vigil on Pigeon Key where they provided shelter to the men who worked the original Florida Overseas Railroad, the boats as they make their way between the Atlantic and Gulf through Money Key and Moser channels, and the mangrove outcroppings that dot the seascape. On a slow traffic day, you will even be rewarded with a glimpse of the lighthouse on the Atlantic side in Hawks Channel.

This poncho was designed in the spirit of the first stingray I saw in the shallow water near Knight Key Channel while I was walking from the Grille out to Pigeon Key. The way the poncho moves when I walk reminds me of the graceful way the sea rays move through the water as they crisscross from the Gulf to the Atlantic.

Reminiscent of gentle undulating waves, this poncho flutters in the breeze as you pedal along through your day in effortless elegance with a smile on your face and a song in your heart.

Universal Yarn Colorburst makes the front of this poncho much easier than it looks. The long color runs of Colorburst present as a series of stripes as they are knit in a two-stitch basket weave for additional visual interest.

Yarn

MC: Universal Yarn Deluxe Worsted Superwash (100% superwash wool); 220 yd/200 m per 3.5 oz/100 g skein; Color: 717 Summer Sky, 4 (5, 5) skeins

CC: Universal Yarn Colorburst (65% superwash merino wool, 35% acrylic); 660 yd/600 m per 7 oz/200 g ball; Color: 109 Spring, 1 ball

Sizes

Small (Medium, Large) to suit a 34 (40, 46)″/86 (102, 117) cm bust measurement; shown in size Small

Dimensions

Small: 46″/117 cm at widest point × 25″/64 cm high Back Panel, 17.5″/45 cm wide × 23″/58 cm high Front Panel
Medium: 52″/132 cm at widest point × 25″/64 cm high Back Panel, 20″/51 cm wide × 23″/58 cm high Front Panel
Large: 58″/147 cm at widest point × 25″/64 cm high Back Panel, 23″/58 cm wide × 23″/58 cm high Front Panel

Gauge

20 sts × 28 rows = 4″/10 cm square in stockinette stitch using Deluxe Worsted Superwash and US size 8/5 mm needle, blocked
26 sts × 30 rows = 4″/10 cm in Woven Basket Stitch using Colorburst and US size 6/4 mm needle, blocked

Needles

US size 8/5 mm circular needle, US size 7/4.5 mm circular needle, US size 6/4 mm straight or circular needle, US size 5/3.75 mm straight or circular needle

Notions

Tapestry needle, 4 locking stitch markers, blocking board, blocking wires, knit blockers

Special Stitch

Woven Basket Stitch (multiple of two stitches):
Row 1 (RS): *Wyib, pass right needle behind first stitch on left needle, knit second stitch on left needle, do not drop either off left needle, knit first stitch on left needle, drop both off the left needle, repeat from * to end of row.
Row 2 (WS): P1, *purl second stitch on left needle, do not drop second stitch off left needle, purl first stitch on left needle, drop both off left needle, repeat from * to last st, p1.

Here I've worked the Woven Basket Stitch in a few different yarns. At top left, Cobblestone by Universal Yarn, next to it Colorburst, and below Colorburst in two additional colorways to see how different colors responded to the stitch and to get a sense of which colors evoked the sense of calm on the Gulf of Mexico that I was seeking for this poncho. In a lighter color the shadow added additional visual interest, so I chose to use a light colorway to provide the additional shadow to the piece.

Pattern Notes

○ In the interest of keeping the knitting less tedious, concentrate on the stitch gauge in the Woven Basket Stitch as it will determine the width of the Front Panel of the finished poncho. The Back, knit side to side, is less reliant on gauge and more on desired finished measurement.

○ The piece is written in three sizes. To scale up the piece, the Front Panel should measure one-half the desired bust measurement and the Back should measure 12″/30.5 cm wider than the desired bust measurement.

Take a break and take it all in, wherever your day may lead. The superwash wool in the Seven Mile Bridge Poncho will keep you comfortable. Working the back in a #4/worsted-weight and the front in a simple basket stitch using a self-striping #3/DK-weight keeps the mundane stockinette quick and the basket stitch fun.

○ I recommend that you use a circular needle for the Back, as the number of stitches may be difficult to work comfortably on a straight set.

○ Depending on how you tension the yarn and hold your needles, you may find it more comfortable to work the Front Panel on a metal needle with a rounded tip. My test knitter and I found it easier to manipulate Colorburst yarn in front of and behind the needle tips of a metal needle. I preferred my Addi Rocket Squared 2 needle; she used an Addi Turbo.

○ To promote a more graceful transition at the shoulder, the Front Panel gauge is tightened a bit by stepping down a needle size for the final six rows.

○ When binding off the Front Panel, the excess yarn specified for the tails, 2.5 yd/2 m, will be used for seaming the pieces together during assembly.

INSTRUCTIONS

Front Panel

Using the US size 5/3.75 mm needle and CC, cast on 114 (132, 150) sts.

Ribbing Row 1 (RS): *K2, p1, repeat from * to end of row.
Ribbing Row 2 (WS): *K1, p2, repeat from * to end of row.

Repeat ribbing rows 1 and 2 a total of two times.

Sizes Small and Large only: Repeat ribbing rows 1 and 2 one more time.

Size Medium only:
Ribbing Row 5: *K2, p1, repeat from * to end of row.
Ribbing Row 6: K2tog, p1, *k1, p2, repeat from * to last 3 sts, k1, p2tog. (2 sts dec)

All sizes:
Using the US size 6/4 mm needle, continue in Woven Basket Stitch (see Special Stitches) until work measures 22″/56 cm from cast-on row or 1″/2.5 cm shorter than desired length, having just finished a WS row.

Lay the work flat.

Place marker to denote the halfway point in the row just completed, 57 (65, 75) sts on either side of marker.

Place marker to denote the neckline ribbing in the row just completed, 30 (38, 48) sts from the right selvedge edge, and the same from the left selvedge edge.

Continue as follows using the US size 5/3.75 mm needle.

There isn't a bad angle to be found.

Neckline Row 1 (RS): Work in Woven Basket Stitch to m, sm, *k2, p1, repeat from * to 3rd m, continue in Woven Basket Stitch.

Neckline Row 2 (WS): Work in Woven Basket Stitch to m, sm, *k1, p2, repeat from * to 3rd m, continue in Woven Basket Stitch.

Repeat Neckline rows 1 and 2 a total of three times.

On the next RS row, bind off between the markers 54 sts in pattern. Continue to end of row in pattern.

WS: Bind off remaining stitches before ribbing, break yarn, leaving a tail of approximately 2.5 yd/2 m. Using working yarn, draw a 2.5 yd/2 m tail, bind off remaining stitches with the working yarn.

Bind-off used: knit 1, pass stitch back to left needle, k2togtbl.

Place locking stitch marker in cast-on row, 57 (65, 75) sts on either side of marker; this will aid in the process of aligning the panels for assembly.

Back/Sleeves

Using MC on the US size 7/4.5 mm needle and the long-tail cast-on method, cast on 126 sts.

Ribbing Row 1 (RS): *K2, p1, repeat from * to end of row.

Ribbing Row 2 (WS): *K1, p2, repeat from * to end of row.

Repeat Ribbing rows 1 and 2 a total of three times.

Using the US size 8/5 mm needle continue as follows:

Row 1 (RS): Sl1, k1, p1, knit to last 3 sts, p1, k2.

Row 2 (WS): Sl1, p1, k1, purl to last 3 sts, k1, p2.

Repeat rows 1 and 2 until piece measures 45 (51, 57)"/114 (130, 145) cm, ending with a WS row.

Using US size 7/4.5 mm needle, repeat Ribbing rows 1 and 2 a total of three times.

Bind off in pattern.

Lay the work flat and place a locking stitch marker along one of the selvedge edges to denote the midpoint along this edge of the rectangle. Place second marker on opposite selvedge edge. These markers will remain in the work during finishing to facilitate alignment of the front and back.

Finishing

Steam block the two panels to the stated dimensions.

Pin to blocking board and allow the pieces to air dry.

Remove the pieces from the blocking board and place the Back with the WS facing and selvedge edge (not cast-on or bind-off edge) parallel to your body as you stand facing it on the work surface.

Place the Front atop the Back with RS facing and the selvedge edges perpendicular to your body.

Align the four midpoint markers (two on the top and two on the bottom).

Using the first tail and a tapestry needle, begin to seam the pieces together from the marker out toward the selvedge edge of the Front. Do not cut the yarn.

Pull the Back upper-right corner down to meet the selvedge edge of the Front, and repeat for upper-left corner.

Pull the Back lower-right corner up to meet the selvedge edge of the Front, and repeat for the lower-left corner.

Pin these pieces in place.

Using tapestry needle, continue to sew down the seam between the selvedge edge of the Front and cast-on edge of the Back; repeat for cast-off edge and remaining shoulder.

Lightly steam the finished poncho.

For a slightly more rounded shoulder seam, turn the work so the right sides are facing each other and sew an auxiliary seam down from a point 1"/2.5 cm in from the corner along the shoulder and 1"/2.5 cm down the side to form a triangle. Turn the work right-side out.

Lightly steam the poncho a second time to settle the auxiliary seam into place.

Revisit ends to make sure none revealed themselves during blocking. If they did, use the tapestry needle to weave them in.

Enjoy your new poncho.

To slightly round the shoulder seam, with RS facing sew an auxiliary seam down from a point 1"/2.5 cm in from the corner along the shoulder and 1"/2.5 cm down the side to form a triangle.

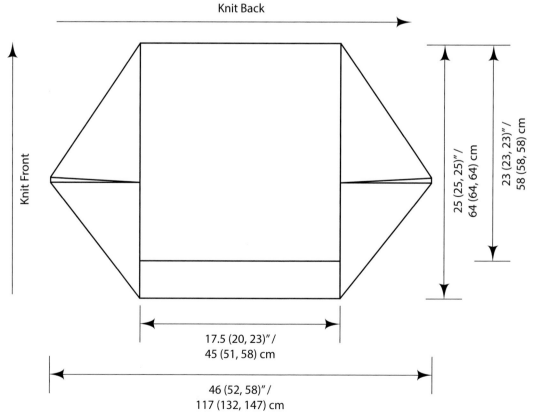

Knit Back

Knit Front

25 (25, 25)" / 64 (64, 64) cm

23 (23, 23)" / 58 (58, 58) cm

17.5 (20, 23)" / 45 (51, 58) cm

46 (52, 58)" / 117 (132, 147) cm

Nantucket Storm Cocoon

When the wind starts to howl and the skies grow dark on a long summer day, you know there's something brewing over the horizon. The shadows become more apparent and the water more menacing as a summer storm builds. This colorway reminds me of how a summer storm looks through the lens of a porthole window out in Buzzards Bay. The deep churning interplay of blues and greens, the waning bits of golden sun giving way to the darkness, and the subtle pops of lightning cresting over the horizon all come together in this coastal palette. So, naturally, it had to become a cozy layer against the sudden chill preceding stormy weather, and the Nantucket Storm Cocoon was born. Knit side to side flat, then seamed and worked in the round, the simple stitch pattern forms the perfect backdrop for this hand-dyed yarn. This one belongs in your closet!

Yarn

Toby Roxanne Designs Beautilitarian DK (100% superwash merino); 250 yd/229 m per 3.5 oz/100 g skein; Color: Summer Storm, 8 (8, 9) skeins

Sizes

Small (Medium, Large); see schematic, shown in Small

Dimensions

58 (62, 66)″/147 (158, 168) cm wingspan, 37″/94 cm, collar to bottom hem

Gauge

20 sts × 28 rows = 4″/10 cm square in k2, p1 ribbing, worked in the round, blocked, using US size 5/3.75 mm needle
24 sts × 30 rows = 4″/10 cm square in pattern stitch, worked flat, blocked, using US size 6/4 mm needle

Needles

US size 6/4 mm 24″/61 cm circular, US size 6/4 mm DPNs or 9″/23 cm circular
US size 5/3.75 mm 30″/76 cm circular, US size 5/3.75 mm DPNs or 9″/23 cm circular

Notions

Tapestry needle, locking stitch marker, US size H/5 mm crochet hook, blocking board, blocking pins

Pattern Notes

o Knit from side to side, this cocoon is designed with no shaping, making it an appealing knit for a beginner and perfect knit for social knitters of any skill level.

o The bodice is a rectangle knit from side to side, then folded, seamed, and trimmed with arms and a collar.

o The design was developed with simple knitting in mind, with as few seams and as few

Page 125: The refined, sumptuous ease with which this cocoon slides on makes you want to wear it.

purl rows as possible without becoming completely boring to knit and wear.

o The nature of the "k2tog" and "kfb" rows keeps the superwash fabric from growing too much when worn. If the swatch feels too loose, and you are concerned about it growing over time, substitute in a "k2togtbl" to tighten up the row gauge. Since the piece is knit side to side, you can knit additional rows to compensate for the slightly more compressed rows.

o For a longer finished garment, add stitches in even increments to maintain pattern repeat.

o The size Small is comprised of a rectangle measuring 24 × 38"/61 × 96 cm, to which the arms are knit from the elbow out, and the collar/edging is picked up. To scale the pieces up or down, measure your gauge versus that presented and increase or decrease the number of stitches necessary to customize to your preferred size.

o The Small used 7.5 skeins of the stated yarn; customization of fit may require more or less yarn, so buy accordingly. An extra skein is always worth the peace of mind.

o When binding off to form the seam at the elbow, if the width of the elbow needs to be wider, bind off fewer stitches and leave more stitches live on each side. Since the pattern repeat takes place over two stitches, always increase by an even number of stitches.

o For a step-by-step refresher on how to work a provisional cast-on, see the Technique Guide on page 36.

The elegant shape of this sweater is given a playful bit of detail by the simple four-row repeat of the pattern stitch, making it the perfect canvas for the hand-dyed yarn to take center stage.

INSTRUCTIONS

Bodice, knit flat

Using scrap yarn, chain 160 sts with the US size H/5 mm crochet hook, place locking stitch marker through the last chain to prevent it from unravelling.

Using a provisional cast-on, and the larger knitting needle, cast on 156 stitches.

Setup row: Purl to end of row.
Row 1 (RS): Knit to end of row.

Celebrate the quiet moments you have to yourself, wrapped up in a warm sweater with a good book and the sunlight streaming in to warm your soul.

Row 2 (WS): K2tog to end of row.
Row 3: Kfb to end of row.
Row 4: Purl to end of row.

Repeat rows 1–4 until piece measures 38 (42, 46)"/96 (107, 117) cm or desired width from elbow to elbow, having just finished a row 4.

Arrange the stitches on the needle such that half of them are on one end of the needle and the other half are on the other half of the needle. With the WS facing, hold the two needles parallel to each other and begin a three-needle bind-off. Bind off until 54 (60, 64) sts remain live. Transition these 54 (60, 64) sts to a stitch holder; they will be used to make the second Sleeve.

Remove the provisional cast-on and transition the work to the longer needle. Arrange the stitches on the needle such that half of them are on one end of the needle and the other half are on the other half of the needle. With the WS facing, hold the two needles parallel to each other and begin a three-needle bind-off. Bind off until 54 (60, 64) sts remain live; these 54 (60, 64) sts will be used to make the first Sleeve.

Sleeves, knit flat

With RS facing, transition the 54 (60, 64) sts to a set of DPNs or 9"/23 cm circular needle of the same size as was used on the Bodice.

Continue in pattern until sleeve measures 10"/25 cm or desired length from approximately the apex of the elbow to the wrist of the person for whom it is being made. End, having completed a row 4.

Transition work to smaller needles and continue in a "k1, p1" rib for four rows.

Bind off in pattern. Using a tapestry needle, seam along selvedge edge of Sleeve.

Repeat for second Sleeve.

Collar/Fronts/Hem Ribbing, knit in the round

With RS facing, and same needle used for the Bodice, pick up 318 (342, 360) sts along the selvedge edges of the work.

Join to work in the round, placing a marker to denote the end of the round.

Begin k2, p1 ribbing and continue for approximately 7½"/19 cm or until desired length is completed. For a custom fit, after 6"/15 cm, place the work onto a piece of scrap yarn and try it on to see how the piece hangs.

When the desired length is completed, bind off in pattern.

Finishing

Wash the finished piece per ball band instructions or gently steam it to relax the fibers.

Revisit ends to make sure none revealed themselves during blocking. If they did, use the tapestry needle to weave them in.

Enjoy your new cocoon.

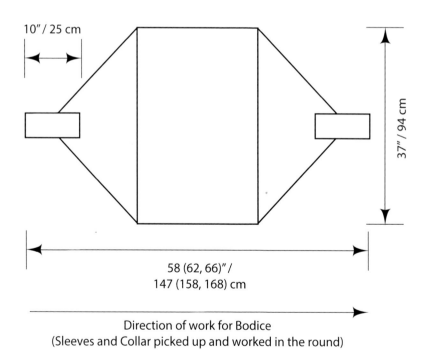

10" / 25 cm

37" / 94 cm

58 (62, 66)" /
147 (158, 168) cm

Direction of work for Bodice
(Sleeves and Collar picked up and worked in the round)

St. Michaels Fog Sweater

$\mathcal{A}$h, the age-old dilemma: what to make for a person who prefers to wear a favorite sweatshirt instead of a gorgeous hand-knit cabled sweater? Rather than fight the natural preference for something simple like a sweatshirt, knit a sweater using a sumptuous, refined yarn that will flow effortlessly from the skein over your needles into a sweater shaped like a sweatshirt with a little tailoring to keep it neat. After spending some serious time asking the men in my life what they do and don't like about various sweaters and sweatshirts they've had, a few themes became apparent to me, and here is the result, the St. Michaels Fog Sweater. Soft, tailored but not tight, sleeve cuff to protect a dive watch, and a bit of built-in stretch to keep the elbows from wearing prematurely make it perfect for those early fall evenings at Foxy's or over at Loves Wharf after a day sail on the Bay.

Pro Tip: When making a swatch for this project, swatch in the round. Stitch gauge can be different when knitting flat or in the round due to the way the yarn is tensioned and the distance the yarn travels to create a knit versus a purl stitch. If you don't like swatching, start the sleeve and measure your gauge about 25 rounds into it. If you get the gauge you want, keep going on the sleeve; if not, pull it out and try again.

Yarn

Pascuali Alpaca Royal (80% alpaca royal, 20% baby alpaca); 145 yd/133 m per 0.88 oz/25 g cake; Color: 068, 18 (20, 27, 28) cakes

Sizes

Small (Medium, Large, XLarge) (see schematic; shown in Medium)

Dimensions

See schematic

Gauge

24 sts × 32 rows = 4"/10 cm square in pattern stitch, blocked, using larger needle

Needles

US size 4/3.5 mm 24"/61 cm circular needle, US size 3/3.25 mm 24"/61 cm circular needle, set of US size 4/3.5 mm and US size 3/3.25 mm DPNs or 9"/22 cm circular needle; for Large or XLarge, 24"/61 cm circular may be too difficult to use, so size your circulars' lengths for comfort while knitting.

Notions

Stitch markers, tapestry needle

When you have the time to relax, reflect, and read the whole newspaper, do it in comfort with a dash of style.

Pattern Notes

- The yarn is held double throughout this project to create an exceptionally warm, light-weight sweater.
- The sweater itself when knit in a larger size may stretch when worn due to the amount of yarn required to make a larger size. To remediate this, apply a single chain false seam on the wrong side of the knit sweater after finishing the sweater along each side of the bodice.
- The sweater is worked up from the hem to the collar in the round for a more flattering athletic fit. For a more generous fit, cast on the number of stitches for the chest rather than the waist and work in pattern with no increases, forming a straight tube from the hem to the chest/underarm.
- Short rows on the Back are added to provide additional ease vertically on the back of the bodice. These rows may be omitted. Short rows do not add a net number of stitches to the rounds; they do add additional length to the piece so the hem remains consistent along its circumference when worn.
- Working in the round can be confusing; to minimize visual confusion, a second marker is introduced to the work to denote the half-way point in the round. To maintain one's orientation when working in the round, it may be helpful to add two locking markers in the field of stockinette stitches after the first ten rounds are worked, one on each side of the piece to denote "Front" and "Back."
- To facilitate tracking the location of the wrapped stitches because the yarn is held double throughout, it may be easier to see the wrapped stitches if, after each one is worked, a locking stitch marker is positioned around the wrap to remind you of the location of each wrapped stitch, as these wrapped stitches are specifically referenced while working the rows.
- The arms of the sweater have a ribbed panel that runs their length to accommodate a range of arm widths.

Pro Tips:

- Any changes to the pattern should be written down to facilitate future projects using the same pattern.
- Sweaters are tough "to-go" projects once they reach that critical size when they no longer fit in one's preferred travel bag. Sleeves are good "to-go" projects, so be sure to make a little room in your weekender bag to work on them after the bodice gets too bulky to tote around.
- When knitting in the round using more than one marker in the work, make note of which one is the end/beginning of round marker, or use a different color marker for this important spot in the work.

The shaping of the raglan sleeve and simple ribbing of the crew neck give this sweater the elegance and sensibility to stand the test of time.

INSTRUCTIONS

Bodice: Ribbed Hem

Using smaller needle and two strands of yarn from two separate cakes held together, cast on 180 (192, 252, 288) sts using a long-tail cast-on. Place marker to denote end of round and join to work in the round.

Round 1: *K2, p2, repeat from * to end of round.

Repeat round 1 12 (12, 14, 14) times.

Bodice, Part One

Transition the work to the larger needle size as you continue in the round.

Sizes Small (Large) only:

First Increase Round: *K18, M1, repeat from * to end of round. (10 [14] sts inc)

Continue knitting rounds with no additional increases until the piece measures 8.5 (10)"/21.5 (25.5) cm from the cast-on edge. (190 [266] sts)

Second Increase Round: *K14, M1, repeat from * to last 8 (–) sts, knit to end of round. (13 [19] sts inc)

Continue knitting rounds with no additional increases until the piece measures 9.5 (11)"/24 (28) cm from the cast-on edge. (203 [285] sts)

Third Increase Round: *K13, M1, repeat from * to last 8 (12) sts, knit to end of round. (15 [21] sts inc)

Continue knitting in rounds with no additional increases until the Bodice measures 12 (13)"/30.5 (33) cm from the cast-on edge. (218 [306] sts)

Place second marker in the work halfway around.

Sizes Medium (XLarge) only:

First Increase Round: *K16, M1, repeat from * to end of round. (12 [18] sts inc)

Continue knitting rounds with no additional increases until the piece measures 9.5"/24 cm from the cast-on edge. (204 [306] sts)

Second Increase Round: *K12, M1, repeat from * to end of round (last 6 sts, knit to end of round). (17 [25] sts inc)

Continue knitting rounds with no additional increases until the piece measures 10.5 (13.5)"/26.5 (34.5) cm from the cast-on edge. (221 [331] sts)

Size Medium only:

Third Increase Round: *K13, M1, repeat from * to end of round. (17 sts inc)

Continue knitting rounds with no additional increases until the piece measures 11.5"/29 cm from the cast-on edge. (238 sts)

Fourth Increase Round: *K17, M1, repeat from * to end of round. (14 sts inc)

Continue knitting in rounds with no additional increases until the Bodice measures 12.5"/32 cm from the cast-on edge. (252 sts)

Place second marker in the work halfway around.

Size XLarge only:

Continue knitting in rounds with no additional increases until the piece measures 13.5"/34.5 cm from the cast-on edge. (331 sts)

Work one additional round until 2 sts remain, k2tog. (330 sts)

Place second marker in the work halfway around.

Bodice: Back

Short Row Shaping for Back of Bodice; see Pattern Notes before proceeding.

Row 1 (RS): K5, wrap and turn.
Row 2 (WS): P5, sm, purl to second marker, sm, p5, wrap and turn.
Row 3 (RS): Knit until 9 sts remain before the wrapped stitch from Row 1, wrap and turn.
Row 4 (WS): Purl until 9 sts remain before the wrapped stitch from Row 2, wrap and turn.
Row 5 (RS): Knit until 9 sts remain before the wrapped stitch from Row 3, wrap and turn.

Subtle shaping from the hem up to the collar makes this sweater customizable as it is knit.

Designed with bespoke detailing from the cuff up, the ribbing provides a comfortable fit without unnecessary bulk to work with the person it envelops. As Ludwig Mies Van Der Rohe was known to say, "Less is more."

Row 6 (WS): Purl until 9 sts remain before the wrapped stitch from Row 3, wrap and turn.

Row 7: Knit to the end of round marker, hiding all wraps and removing the wrap markers as you come to them.

Next round: Knit, hiding all wraps and removing wrap markers as you come to them.

Check the stitch count and verify that the second marker placed prior to starting the short rows is still marking the halfway point in the work.

Continue knitting in the round until the front half measures 13 (13.5, 14, 14.5)"/33 (34.5, 35.5, 37) cm.

Size Medium only:
Final Increase Round: K2, *k25, M1, repeat from * to end of round. (10 sts inc, 262 sts)

All sizes:
Continue knitting in the round until the front half measures 14 (14.5, 15, 15.5)"/35.5 (37, 38, 39.5) cm.

Set Bodice aside and work on Sleeves.

Cuffs, Sleeves (Make Two)

Using smaller circular needle in shorter diameter or DPNs, cast on 56 sts, place marker, and join in the round.

Cuff Round 1: *K2, p2, repeat from * to end of round.

Repeat round 1 11 (11, 15, 15) additional times.

Sleeve Round 1: Transition work to larger needle as you knit 42 sts, pm, p2, k2, p2, k2, p2, k2, p2. This establishes the pattern that will be maintained along the underside of each arm. The ribbing as presented forms a panel to maintain an athletic fit up the length of the arm.

Sleeve Rounds 2–6: Knit to marker, sm, p2, k2, p2, k2, p2, k2, p2.

Sleeve Round 7: M1L, knit to marker, M1R, sm, p2, k2, p2, k2, p2, k2, p2. (2 sts inc)

Repeat rounds 2–7 an additional 24 times. (50 sts inc total from cuff)

Continue in pattern with no additional increases until Sleeve measures 20 (20, 21, 21)"/51 (51, 53.5, 53.5) cm or desired length to underarm where it will meet the Bodice. (106 sts)

Bodice, Part Two

Knit in the round until 7 stitches before the midpoint marker. Place 14 sts onto a piece of scrap yarn or stitch holder. Move the marker to the last Bodice stitch worked. Working with the Sleeve stitches, incorporate 92 knit stitches from the Sleeve into this round of the Bodice, place marker to denote the last Sleeve stitch after it is incorporated into the Bodice, place the remaining 14 Sleeve sts (the ribbed portion of the Sleeve) on a stitch holder or piece of scrap yarn. Continue knitting Bodice stitches until 7 stitches remain, place marker. Place these 7 and first 7 from the next round onto a piece of scrap yarn or stitch holder. Remove the end of round marker. Working with the Sleeve stitches, incorporate the 92 knit stitches from the Sleeve into this round of the Bodice, place the remaining 14 Sleeve stitches (the ribbed stitches) on a stitch holder or piece of scrap yarn. Return the beginning/end of round marker to the work after the last of the 92 knit stitches from the second Sleeve are knit onto the Bodice.

Four markers are now in the work. These will be used to facilitate the decreases as the piece is worked in the round to the neckline. The markers denote the points at which the Sleeves have been joined to the work. If all four are the same color, mark the fourth one as the end of round marker to facilitate counting rows for yoke and ribbing.

Yoke

Rounds 1–3: Knit.
Rounds 4–7: *K1, k2tog, k to 3 sts from m, ssk, k1, sm, repeat from * to end of round. (8 sts dec)
Round 8: Knit.

Repeat rounds 7 and 8 a total of 29 (34, 39, 43) times. (110 [114, 112, 110] sts)

Sizes Small and XLarge final yoke round:

Knit to m, sm, k1, k2tog, knit to 3 stitches from end of round, ssk, k1. (2 sts dec)

Size Medium final yoke round:

Knit to m, sm, k1, k2tog, knit to 3 sts from m, ssk, k1, sm, k1, k2tog, knit to 3 sts before m, k2tog, k1, sm, k1, ssk, knit to 3 stitches from end of round, ssk, k1. (6 sts dec)

Yoke Ribbing

Transition work to smaller needle as you work the next round.

Round 1: *K2, p2, repeat from * to end of round.
Rounds 2–7: Repeat round 1.

Bind off using a stretchy bind-off.

Finishing

Weave in ends.

Steam the 28 stitches under each arm to facilitate seaming. Return the 2 sets of 14 sts to needles, and seam using Kitchener stitch.

Steam block finished sweater to relax the stitches and block to final dimensions while the fabric is still damp. Allow to air dry.

Revisit ends to make sure none revealed themselves during blocking. If they did, use the tapestry needle to weave them in.

Enjoy your new sweater.

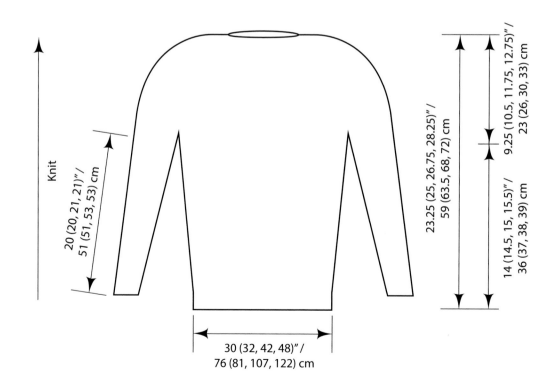

Knit

20 (20, 21, 21)" /
51 (51, 53, 53) cm

23.25 (25, 26.75, 28.25)" /
59 (63.5, 68, 72) cm

9.25 (10.5, 11.75, 12.75)" /
23 (26, 30, 33) cm

14 (14.5, 15, 15.5)" /
36 (37, 38, 39) cm

30 (32, 42, 48)" /
76 (81, 107, 122) cm

Santa Monica Shell

ever one to settle for another boring silk shell that has to be ironed or professionally cleaned, I prefer to knit them myself out of interesting washable yarns to create an uncluttered silhouette that complements a pair of jeans or a sumptuous suede skirt.

This is a true coast-to-coast project. The yarn, Blue Heron Rayon Metallic, is hand-dyed in small batches in Delaware. I found it first in a shop in St. Michaels, Maryland, while enjoying their annual Christmas Stroll. The way the colors dance along the yarn, reflecting the light in different ways to create a calming palette, reminded me of the sandy beach in Santa Monica where I like to run in the mornings when I am fortunate enough to be in LA. There's a wonderful path right along the beach; the sand blows gently across it when the wind is right. One can run, cycle, stroll, or simply sit and enjoy the view of the ocean as the sun creates a sparkly path to it while the palm trees sway gently in the background.

Blue Heron Rayon Metallic is the perfect yarn for this project because it comes in a wide range of colors, is easy to take care of, and a pleasure with which to knit. Garments knit out of Blue Heron Rayon Metallic evoke a sense of effortless elegance.

In short, you will find this to be the perfect tank top for layering for a brunch date or for a night out on the town, any time of year.

Yarn

Blue Heron Rayon Metallic (85% rayon, 15% metallic); 550 yd/502 m per 8 oz/227 g skein; Color: Polar Bear, 1 (2, 2, 2, 2) skeins

Sizes

32 (34, 36, 38, 42)"/81 (86, 91, 97, 107) cm bust, finished garment will have approximately 1"/2.5 cm negative ease to fit these sizes; shown in 34"/86 cm

Dimensions

See schematic

Gauge

22 sts and 28 rows = 4"/10 cm square in stockinette stitch, worked in the round, blocked, using US 6/4 mm needle

Needles

US size 6/4 mm 24 or 32"/60 or 81 cm circular; US size 5/3.75 mm 24 or 32"/60 or 81 cm circular, 16"/40 cm circular or DPNs. Note: circular needle length based on garment size and knitter's preference.

Notions

Tapestry needle, cable needle, 4 stitch markers, 4 stitch holders or scrap yarn, 2 colorfast bath towels, blocking board

Page 137: Be at the top of your game in this shell as you move effortlessly around the party on the deck before a night on the town.

Special Stitches

Edge Stitch:
Work all edging with WS facing as follows in the round:

Round 1 (WS): Knit.

Round 2: *Sl1 with yarn held on RS, k1, repeat from * to end of round.

Round 3: *Sl1 with yarn held on RS, p1, repeat from * to end of round.

Round 4: Knit.

Cast off all stitches knitwise through the back of the loop.

C2F (cable 2 front): Sl1 st to cable needle, hold to front, k1, k1 from cable needle.

Pattern Notes

- Rayon Metallic can be difficult to wind. Wind it by hand with the assistance of another person to hold the hank aloft, or drape it over the back of a chair to wind from the hank into a ball—not a center-pull ball. It is easiest to work the yarn from the outside of the ball rather than the center. To further aid in preventing the yarn from becoming entangled, place the ball of yarn in a plastic zip-top bag or yarn caddy.

- Stitch gauge is more important than row gauge, as the fabric has a fluid hand and will form itself to the body.

- This top is worked in the round to the armhole, at which point the back and front are worked separately and seamed using a three-needle bind-off at the shoulder prior to working the trim.

- When shaping, the bust increases are only done on the front. The straps are designed to present at a bit of an angle along the back to enhance the female form.

- When shaping the armholes and neckline, the stitches are not bound off; they are slipped to a holder or scrap yarn so the live stitches may be used, in combination with picked-up stitches, to work the border edging. Using the live stitches and slipped stitches creates a smoother transition between the two than picking up bound-off stitches.

- All slipped stitches are slipped as if to purl throughout unless otherwise noted.

- Two needle sizes are used for this tank top. When working the cabled band, it is easier to transition to the bodice because the two different needle sizes create less of a horizontal line as the stitches transition from the ribbed cable to the stockinette. When blocked, the cabled band is slightly stretched horizontally, will hug the hips when worn and minimize gapping.

- When neck stitches and armhole stitches are completed, these openings will be tightened up. Therefore, the measurements for the armholes may seem too large as you knit them, but they will close up based on the number of stitches for which the edge stitch is used.

- Increases to enhance the bust are done where needed, beneath the widest part of the bust rather than simply along the seams, so as to maintain a smoother line across the back to minimize gapping under the arm or along the shoulder.

- No two bodies are exactly the same size. To be more inclusive, sizing is proportional throughout the piece—the wider the bust, the longer the finished top. If a shorter version is desired, decrease the number of rows worked without shaping. For a long, slim torso, increase the number of rows worked without shaping. For optimal results, changes to the length should be made after the cabling of the hem and before the bust shaping.

- For a refresher on how to work the three-needle-bind off, see the Technique Guide on page 37.

INSTRUCTIONS

Bodice, knit in the round from the hem up

With smaller needle, cast on 90 (96, 102, 108, 114) sts, pm, cast on 90 (96, 102, 108, 114) sts, pm, join in the round. (180 [192, 204, 216, 228] sts)

Rounds 1–10: *K4tbl, p2, repeat from * to end of round.

Round 11: *C2F, p2tbl, repeat from * to end of round.

Rounds 12–15: Repeat round 1.

Round 16: Repeat round 11.

Repeat rounds 12–16 three more times.

Repeat rounds 1–8.

Switch to larger needles.

Work even in stockinette stitch in the round until piece measures 5.5 (6, 6.5, 7.5, 8)″/14 (15, 16.5, 19, 20) cm from cast-on edge.

Bodice Decreases

Round 1: Ssk, knit to 2 sts before m, k2tog, sm, ssk, knit to 2 sts before m, k2tog. (4 sts dec) (176 [188, 200, 212, 224] sts)

Rounds 2–7: Knit.

Repeat rounds 1–7 four more times. (80 [86, 92, 98, 104] sts remaining between each marker)

Work even without shaping until piece measures 10.5 (11, 11.5, 12.5, 13)″/27 (28, 28, 32, 33) cm from cast-on edge.

Insert markers into the work so there is a marker 20 stitches from the first marker and a second 20 stitches in front of the next marker. These two sets of 20 stitches represent the points inside which the bust shaping will take place. The markers will have 38 (44, 50, 56, 62) sts between them. Shaping will also take place at the beginning of the round and midpoint of the round, the Front of the tank top.

Bust Shaping

Round 1: K20, sm, k1, M1L, knit to 1 st before m, M1R, k1, sm, k20, knit to end of round. (2 sts inc on Front, 82 [88, 94, 100, 106] sts for Front; 80 [86, 92, 98, 104] sts for Back)

Rounds 2–5: Knit.

Round 6: M1L, knit to m, sm, k1, M1L, knit to 1 st before next m, M1R, k1, sm, knit to m, M1R, knit to end of round. (4 sts inc on Front, 86 [92, 98, 104, 110] sts for Front; 0 sts inc on Back, 80 [86, 92, 98, 104] sts for Back)

Rounds 7–11: Knit.

Sizes 38 (42)″/96.5 (106.5) cm only: Repeat rounds 2–6 one (two) times. (108 [118] sts Front)

All sizes:

Rounds 12–21: Repeat rounds 1–10. (92 [98, 104, 114, 124] sts Front; 80 [86, 92, 98, 104] sts Back)

Rounds 21–26: Repeat rounds 1–5. (94 [100, 106, 116, 126] sts Front; 80 [86, 92, 98, 104] sts Back)

Round 27: Knit to m, k2tog, knit to m, ssk, knit to end of round. (2 sts dec on Front, 92 [98, 104, 114, 124] sts Front; 80 [86, 92, 98, 104] sts Back)

Rounds 28–31: Knit.

Round 32: Repeat round 27. (90 [96, 102, 112, 122] sts Front, 80 [86, 92, 98, 104] sts Back)

Sizes 38 (42)″/96.5 (106.5) cm only: Repeat rounds 27–31 one (two) times. (110 [118] sts)

All sizes: Work even without shaping until piece measures 16 (16, 17, 19, 21)″/41 (41, 43, 48, 56) cm from cast-on edge.

Shape Armholes Front, knit flat

Row 1 (RS): Remove marker and clip it to the last st of Back, knit to 6 (6, 8, 10, 10) sts from second m, transition stitches worked to a stitch holder, k6 (6, 8, 10, 10), sm, knit to third marker, sm, k6 (6, 8, 10, 10), turn work. (12 [12, 16, 20, 20] sts dec)

Row 2 (WS): Purl. (78 [84, 86, 92, 102] sts)

Row 3: Sl2 to stitch holder, knit to end of row.
Row 4: Sl2 to stitch holder, purl to end of row.

Repeat rows 3 and 4, slipping 2 stitches at the beginning of each row unworked to the stitch holder, until 54 (60, 72, 88, 98) sts remain.

Continue in pattern without decreasing until armhole measures approximately. 5 (5, 6, 6, 6)"/13 (13, 15, 15, 15) cm, ending with Row 3.

Move center 16 (20, 24, 28, 30) sts to spare circular needle or scrap yarn; use a piece about 36"/91.5 cm in length as it will be used to hold other live stitches as you work the neckline. (19 [20, 24, 30, 34] sts each side, which will be worked for the shoulders)

Shape Neck at Left Front Shoulder, knit flat

Row 1 (WS): Sl1, purl to end of row. (19 [20, 24, 30, 34] sts)
Row 2 (RS): Sl2 to scrap yarn, knit to end of row. (17 [18, 22, 28, 32] sts remain to be worked on next row)
Row 3: Sl1, purl to 1 st from end of row, sl1 to scrap yarn. (16 [17, 21, 27, 31] sts remain to be worked on next row)
Row 4: Sl2 to scrap yarn, knit to end of row. (14 [15, 19, 25, 29] sts remain to be worked on next row)
Row 5: Sl1, purl to 1 st from end of row, sl1 to scrap yarn. (13 [14, 18, 24, 28] sts remain to be worked on next row)
Row 6: Sl2 to scrap yarn, knit to 2 sts from end of row, k2tog. (10 [11, 15, 21, 25] sts remain to be worked on next row)
Row 7: S1, purl to 1 st from end of row, sl1 to scrap yarn. (9 [10, 14, 20, 24] sts remain to be worked on next row)

Work 8 rows or until desired length without shaping, knitting and purling sts as presented, slipping the first stitch of each row.

The subtle shaping keeps this top aligned to help you look and feel your best.

Place remaining 9 (10, 14, 20, 24) sts on holder; these will be used for the three-needle bind-off to form the shoulder seam. Leave a 39"/99 cm tail.

Work neck at Right Front Shoulder, reversing shaping, using same number of stitches on the Right Front Shoulder.

Move remaining Front sts to scrap yarn or stitch holder. Cut yarn, leaving 39"/99 cm tail.

From every angle, this shell shines and catches you in the best possible light. From the delicate cabled hem to the last stitches completed at the neckline, it is simple and elegant.

Shaping Armholes Back, knit flat

Note: There are fewer stitches on the Back, as increases for bust were done only on the Front. This creates a nicer frame for the shoulder blades and lies flatter along the Back, so as to present with minimal or no gapping between the knit fabric and back of the person wearing it.

With RS facing, begin using same yarn and continue as follows only on the Back stitches, slipping stitches to scrap yarn as indicated.

Row 1 (RS): Beginning at the end of the stitches that comprised row 1 of the Front, knit to the half-way marker, sm, knit across the Back to the stitch that has the end-of-round marker through it—it is now the end of row. Remove the end-of-row marker.

Row 2 (WS): Sl1, purl to halfway marker, turn work and place all remaining stitches onto scrap yarn or stitch holder. Remove the halfway marker.

Row 3: Sl1, knit to end of row.

Row 4: Sl1 to scrap yarn, sl1, purl to last st, sl1 to scrap yarn or stitch holder.

Row 5: Sl1 to scrap yarn, knit across to last st, sl1 to scrap yarn or stitch holder.

Row 6: Sl2 to scrap yarn, purl to last st, sl1 to scrap yarn or stitch holder.

Row 7: Sl2 to scrap yarn, knit to end of row.

Row 8: P2tog, purl to 2 sts from end, ssp. (2 sts dec)

Row 9: Sl1, knit to end of row.

Row 10: Sl1, purl to end of row.

Row 11: Sl1, k2tog, knit to 3 sts from end, ssk, k1. (2 sts dec)

Row 12: Sl1, purl to end of row.

Row 13: Sl1, knit to end of row.

Repeat rows 12–13 with no further shaping, ending with row 13 when Back measures 1"/2.5 cm shorter than Front.

Back Neck Shaping, knit flat

Place center 24 (30, 30, 36, 36) sts on shorter circular needle or two DPNs with stoppers; these will be the neck stitches.

Working with the remaining stitches on each side, begin with the Left Back Shoulder shaping:

Row 1 (RS): Knit to neck sts, turn work.

Row 2 (WS): Sl2 to circular needle, purl to end of row.

Row 3: Sl1, knit to 5 sts from end of row, slip these 5 sts to circular needle.

Row 4: Sl2 to circular needle, purl to end of row.

Continue decreasing in pattern until 9 (10, 14, 20, 24) sts remain.

Place these 9 (10, 14, 20, 24) sts on holder.

Work Right Back Shoulder same as Left Back Shoulder, reversing shaping.

With RS facing each other and using the three-needle bind-off, bind off all sts.

Finishing

Sew side seams. Weave in ends.

Transfer Front Left and Back Left Shoulder sts to DPNs. With RS facing each other and using the three-needle bind-off, bind off 9 (10, 14, 20, 24) sts.

Repeat on right side.

Pick up total of 92 (98, 98, 104, 104) sts along neckline on the smaller circular needle (pick up sts includes a combination of the live sts off the scrap yarn and slipped sts along the neckline). If there are gaps, pick up extra sts on the first round and decrease as necessary to begin edging. Place marker to denote end of round.

Use Edge Stitch pattern (see Special Stitches) to complete the neckline.

Pick up 86 (90, 90, 94, 98) sts around the left armhole (pick up sts includes a combination of slipped sts and live sts off the scrap yarn). To eliminate gapping, pick up extra sts on this first round and decrease if necessary to begin edging. Place marker to denote end of round.

Use Edge Stitch pattern to complete the armhole.

Repeat for right armhole.

Blocking is accomplished by resting the top in a sink of warm water at 110° F. When the top sinks into the basin, allow it to sit for approximately 20 minutes.

Remove it from the basin, unfurl it, and place it between two bath towels. Beginning at one edge, roll the three layers and squeeze the rolled-up set of three layers to release some of the water.

Block it and allow to air dry.

Revisit ends to make sure none revealed themselves during blocking. If they did, use the tapestry needle to weave them in.

Enjoy your new top.

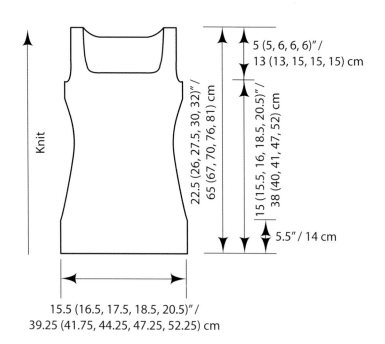

Knit

22.5 (26, 27.5, 30, 32)" / 65 (67, 70, 76, 81) cm

5 (5, 6, 6, 6)" / 13 (13, 15, 15, 15) cm

15 (15.5, 16, 18.5, 20.5)" / 38 (40, 41, 47, 52) cm

5.5" / 14 cm

15.5 (16.5, 17.5, 18.5, 20.5)" / 39.25 (41.75, 44.25, 47.25, 52.25) cm

Oyster Bay Skirt

You know that perfect day when you have time to yourself and just want to get away, carefree for a few hours? Next time you need a break, head out to the "end of the line" on the Long Island Rail Road to the charming seaside village of Oyster Bay, New York, to channel your inner Gatsby, Gold Coast style. Paired with suede boots, this skirt and a cuddly oversized sweater, you're ready to relax with a cup of coffee from Southdown Coffee in one hand and a bagel from IT Bagel in the other as you wander the lovely boutiques and bookshops of Oyster Bay.

Yarn

Pascuali Balayage (80% baby alpaca, 20% organic superfine merino wool); 190 yd/175 m per 1.75 oz/50 g cake; Color: 605, 6 (8, 8) cakes

Sizes

Hips: 34 (37, 40)"/86 (94, 101) cm; Length: 17"/43 cm (see schematic; shown in size 34"/86 cm)

Gauge

22 sts and 30 rows = 4"/10 cm square in stockinette stitch, stitch, worked in the round, unblocked, using US size 6/4 mm needle

Needles

US size 4/3.5 mm 24"/61 cm circular for ribbing, US size 5/3.75 mm 24"/61 cm circular for hem, US size 6/4 mm 24"/61 cm circular for body of skirt (29"/74 cm circular may be more comfortable for larger sizes)

Notions

Tapestry needle, point protectors, locking stitch markers—one unique stitch marker to denote end of round and one per pleat: 14 (16, 17), elastic thread, and sewing needle (optional), 2 colorfast bath towels

Special Stitches

Hem Rib:
Round 1: **[Wyib sl1 st knitwise, move yarn to RS, purl], repeat three times, *yarn to front, sl1 purlwise, k1, repeat from * a total of seven times, repeat from ** to end of the round.
Rounds 2–4: ** *With yarn in front of work, p1, move yarn to back of work, slip 1, repeat from * a total of three times, k1, with yarn in front, slip 1 purlwise, repeat from ** to end of round.

M1: Invisible Lifted Increase (from *Vogue Knitting: The Ultimate Knitting Book*, 7th edition):

Turn the left needle toward you so you can see the purl side of the stitch on the tip of the left needle.

Easygoing does not take effort; it takes imagination. The pleasures of a hand-knit garment should not be restricted to tops. Take the experience to the next logical level: a comfortable skirt perfect for a weekend excursion.

Insert the tip of the right needle from the top down into the stitch below this one.

Wrap working yarn as if to knit, knit this stitch.

Knit stitch on the tip of the left needle.

Continue working in the round.

Pattern Notes

- Knit in the round from the waist down to the hem.
- Two skeins of yarn are worked simultaneously, held double throughout the work, to provide the additional warmth that doubling this yarn provides.
- For a more roomy back or front, use short rows before beginning the pleating and either return to stated numbers before beginning pleating or modify the dimensions of the pleats to suit the preferred number of stitches.

- Each pleat presents with 15 knit stitches separated by one to six purl stitches.
- When increasing using the Invisible Lifted Increase (see Special Stitches), increases look best when done every fourth or more rows. If stacked on fewer rows, the work will tend to pucker. This stitch was selected so as to present the least visual distraction from the stockinette and beautiful hand of this yarn.
- Markers are used to denote the first stitch of the purl ridge of each pleat.
- The Hem stitch is worked over an even number of stitches on a needle one size smaller than that used on the body of the work. When transitioning to the smaller needle, reduce the number of stockinette stitches by one on the front of each pleat to maintain the even number needed for the hem.

INSTRUCTIONS

Using smallest needle size and yarn held doubled, cast on 126 (138, 150) sts.

Join, pm to denote end of round.

Work in "k1, p1" rib for 2"/5 cm.

Hips

Transition sts to largest needle as the next round is worked as follows:

Round 1: *K1, sl1 as if to knit, repeat from * to end of round.

Round 2: See size specific instructions below:

Size Small only: K2tog, knit to end of round. (125 sts)

Size Medium only: Kfb, k68 kfb, knit to end of round. (140 sts)

Size Large only: Knit to end of round. (150 sts)

Rounds 3 and 4: Knit.

Round 5: *K4, M1, k1, repeat from * to end of round. (150 [168, 180] sts)

Continue in the round until work measures 3.25"/8.25 cm with no additional increases.

Inc Round: *K5, M1, k1* to end of round. (175 [196, 210] sts)

Continue in round until work measures 5"/13 cm.

Inc Round: *K6, M1, k1* to end of round. (200 [224, 240] sts)

Continue in round until work measures 8.5"/22 cm.

Inc Round: *K7, M1, k1* to end of round. (225 [252, 270] sts)

Knit three rounds.

Size Medium only: Knit one round, increasing evenly 3 sts. (255 sts)

All sizes: Continue knitting in the round with no additional increases until work measure 10"/25 cm or desired length at which pleats should begin; this point should be below the widest point of hips so the pleats do not open up when worn. (225 [255, 270] sts)

The detail at the top of each pleat and the hem helps the skirt maintain its simple silhouette for the wanderings your weekend itinerary may hold in store.

Pleats

Place marker every 15 sts.

Pleat Increase Round 1: *K15, M1p, repeat from * to end of round. (15 [17, 18] sts inc)

Continue knitting and purling stitches in the round as you come to them until work measures 11"/28 cm.

Pleat Increase Round 2: *K15, p1, M1p, repeat from * to end of round. (15 [17, 18] sts inc)

Continue knitting and purling stitches in the round as you come to them until work measures 13"/33 cm.

Pleat Increase Round 3: *K15, p1, M1p, p1, repeat from * to end of round. (15 [17, 18] sts inc)

Continue knitting and purling stitches in the round as you come to them until work measures 14"/36 cm.

Pleat Increase Round 4: *K15, p3, M1p, repeat from * to end of round. (15 [17, 18] sts inc)

Continue knitting and purling stitches in the round as you come to them until work measures 15"/38.5 cm.

Pleat Increase Round 5: *K15, p3, M1p, p1, repeat from * to end of round. (15 [17, 18] sts inc)

Continue knitting and purling stitches in the round as you come to them until work measures 16"/38.5 cm.

Pleat Increase Round 6: *K15, p5, M1p, repeat from * to end of round. (15 [17, 18] sts inc)

Continue knitting and purling stitches in the round as you come to them until work measures 16.75"/42.5 cm.

Hem

Transition work to medium size needle as the following setup round is worked.

Setup Round: *Knit to 2 sts before m, k2tog, sm, purl to m, sm, repeat from * to end of round.

Work Hem Rib (see Special Stitches).

Bind off as follows: K1, slip st back to left needle, k2togtbl, slip st back to left needle, k2togtbl to the purl ridge, in the purl ridge k2tog rather than tbl.

Finishing

Weave in ends.

Optional: If desired, weave elastic thread through the ribbed waistband to create a snugger fit. Blocking is accomplished by laying the skirt in a sink of warm water at 110° F.

Remove it from the sink, and place it between two bath towels. Beginning at one edge, roll the three layers and squeeze the rolled-up set of three layers to release some of the water.

Block flat and allow to air dry.

Revisit ends to make sure none revealed themselves during blocking. If they did, use the tapestry needle to weave them in.

Enjoy your new skirt.

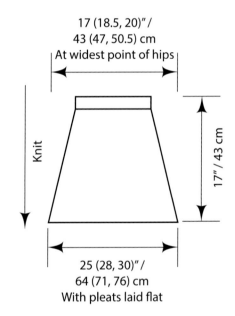

17 (18.5, 20)" /
43 (47, 50.5) cm
At widest point of hips

Knit

17" / 43 cm

25 (28, 30)" /
64 (71, 76) cm
With pleats laid flat

Acknowledgments

In 2016 my friend and mentor, Lars Rains, signed a copy of his book *Modern Lopi* for me. I don't have to open it to tell you what he wrote: "Can't wait to see your book next!" For five years it sat on my desk in silent vigil, reminding me that one day I really did need to get my act together and commit my ideas to paper. In 2020, while pivoting my business to respond to the changing world dynamic, I got out a sketch pad and got to work. Thank you, Lars, for your encouragement and guidance in my darkest moments of self-doubt.

The process of writing this book during the global slowdown proved that with a good team, anything is possible. I am fortunate to have a network of colleagues with whom I was able to work remotely to bring this collection together across the miles. I am exceptionally fortunate that everyone is still speaking to me and each other.

I am grateful for the test knitters who worked tirelessly to get samples knit, provided feedback, and ensured that their finished work was picture-perfect. I could not have done this without you: Julie Sullivan, Zaida Stuart, Angela Monserrate, Denise Sterzel, Maddy Sgueglia, and Liz Novak.

Since we could not gather in person to discuss patterns, yarn pairings, and colors, I knew I needed people I could trust to get the yarn out to the test and sample knitters in a timely fashion. My first call was to my local yarn store, Knit, in Roslyn, New York, where Cheryl Lavenhar stepped right up to help. FaceTime camera in hand, she walked me through the store to find the perfect collection of Cozy Color Works from fellow New York native Sandy Anderson, who was instrumental in dyeing and quickly delivering yarn to Cheryl for distribution. Thank you both for your teamwork.

I considered myself truly fortunate for the support my project received from Universal Yarn. When I called Rachel Brockman at Universal Yarn to tell her about my book ideas, she worked with me for hours via videoconference to pick out just the right yarns for each concept. Thank you, Rachel, Aubrey Busek, and Yonca Ozbelli for the handwritten notes you included in each shipment. I still have them on my desk next to the Universal Yarn measuring tape to remind me that I'm not alone in my quest to bring beautiful yarns together with designs to create timeless pieces of wearable fiber art.

Partnering with a single company was not feasible during the development of this book due to supply chain issues. During my tenure as a consultant, I had the opportunity to travel and visit many yarn stores along the way, where I discovered other exceptional yarns that also appear in this book. The rich, deep colors of Toby Roxane Barna's line of hand-dyed yarns provided the perfect backdrop for a simple textured stitch.

The exceptional hand of the Pascuali Yarns was perfect to take three of the designs herein from sketch pad to finished pattern. And, of course, the rare

The first shipment of yarn from Universal Yarn was very exciting and a bit intimidating until I saw the handwritten note inside to remind me that I had a lot of people ready to help with my project. After only seeing the yarns through several videoconferences, holding the yarns in person made the whole project spring to life.

Toby Roxane's Summer Storm. I was so happy when her yarn arrived. It was a perfect match to the skein with which I had swatched the Nantucket Cocoon. It is a staple in her line. I had bought some after the last lecture she gave to the Long Island Knitting Guild.

treat that is Blue Heron Rayon Metallic—picking just two designs featuring it was difficult.

Thank you to the team at Darn Good Yarn led by Nicole Snow. Amanda Schermerhorn and Alex Bucciferro, you went above and beyond to make sure that the yarns got where they needed to be despite the best efforts of the supply chain to stop you.

After the knitting was done, there were countless hours spent going through what felt like endless piles of clothes. Thank you Cynthia Anderson for helping me style the finalists for the photo shoot and for your professional input on the design of the cover; I never could have put into words what you put into living color. There's no way I'd have gotten through that stack of styling without your help.

I don't know if or when I would have started knitting had it not been for the suggestion of Nancy Benchimol. She suggested I take it on as a hobby when my husband bought a boat. Mrs. B, you were right, knitting is a great hobby for people on the move, whether by land or sea. I'm looking forward to visiting the Monday afternoon knitting group at the Gold Coast Library next time I am in port.

There are two adamant non-knitters who also deserve recognition for their help: my mother, Barbara Palermo, for listening to me drone on endlessly about the minutiae of yarn; and my husband, Erik Fleischauer, for his help keeping the rest of our lives on track for the past two years. Without your help, I'd still be sitting in my office staring at a really big box of yarn.

To all the husbands, wives, boyfriends, girlfriends, and roommates who live in a house full of yarn and spend more than their fair share of time in yarn shops, believe me, your knitting companion appreciates your patience and support.